Girl on the Prow

Also by Sara Jeanne Duncan Widness

The Dusky Afternoon: An Oregon Childhood

Stepping into Somewhere: Family Matters

Available through Bookshop.org,
and anywhere books are sold

Girl on the Prow

Sara Jeanne Duncan Widness

Distinction Press
Waitsfield, Vermont

Distinction Press
Waitsfield, Vermont 05673
www.distinctionpress.com

Girl on the Prow

Cover photography courtesy of Thomas Wilmer.
Poetry by Sara Jeanne Duncan Widness.

ISBN 978-1-937667-23-8 tradepaper
ISBN 978-1-937667-31-3 ebook

Library of Congress Control Number: 2023903467

To my Daughters and Grandson
and Dearest Friends
who weathered the storms with
this girl on the prow
riding high on the roll of the sea ...

From Romberg & Hammerstein's
The New Moon

Let me be like the girl on the prow
Riding high on the roll of the sea …

Dream Snatcher

Dreams seem to be the norm for some. Not for me. I was always so busy keeping up with what the real world threw at me that I had no time for dreams. Sure, as a young girl I fantasized about becoming the girl on the prow who rides high o'er the waves of the sea. I wanted to be that carved and curvaceous wooden figurehead gracing schooners and sailing ships of yore. Most important, though, was the reality that the girl on the prow was always at front and center of the action. On more than one occasion I chose to stand outside on the deck of the Staten Island Ferry begging gale-force winds to help with my fantasy. For minutes on end I became that girl in Sigmund Romberg's *The New Moon*. However, simply by living, the proverbial waves did crash on me, relentlessly.

Bucket lists? Not even in the equation. As a working and single mother, I counted myself fortunate if the current month's income covered the mortgage and food. After life's necessities were addressed and I had any pittance left, I felt lucky to be able to walk into a bookstore to buy a few paperback books or into a pharmacy to select a preferred cologne. Why didn't I use the library instead? The hassle of locating borrowed books to be returned and then dealing with library fines was overwhelming. I sewed my own clothes and dresses, and coats and dresses for the girls. I remember the day I walked into a dress shop in Rutland, Vermont, and purchased a dress that fit me perfectly. It bore the then-prestigious Lanz label. Justifying this purchase kept me awake over more than one night. My argument was that my husband used to buy suits. He was a professional man. I was now a professional. Didn't I deserve this kind of caring too? The dress was successful, sort of, but the wraparound skirt I found so attractive in the dress shop was a nuisance because I could never secure it to achieve modesty. On or off the ship, the wind had its way.

Was being the proprietor of a public relations company a dream? Never. But my employment track record indicated that going it on my own would provide more job security than working for somebody else, which had seldom worked. Public relations was what l knew. I also was a journalist, but supporting my family on the salary of a newspaper reporter was as unrealistic as any dream.

Was I dreaming to steer, in just a few years, first Sara Widness Communications and then a second company to just short of $1 million in revenues before 9/11? This achievement wasn't even a goal — and most certainly not a dream — but the result of day after day putting one foot in front of the other.

Many guests upon arriving at the Fan House, my small inn in Barnard, Vermont, share with me that their dream has always been to own a bed and breakfast. Wouldn't that be fun! Sometimes I respond that they are welcome to return and pinch hit for me as bed and breakfast host. One winter while recovering from simultaneous bunion and eye surgeries, I greeted guests at the door on crutches and with a patch over one eye. "Welcome to the participatory B&B!" I exclaimed. While brandishing crutches, I advised that if they wanted breakfast, guests would need to play a critical role in carrying dishes and food to and from the dining table.

For me living in Barnard in the Fan House was never a dream. Buying the house and transforming the structure into one that would produce income were calculated moves. Saying farewell to Manhattan and the sybaritic world to which I was at risk of becoming too accustomed was not a dream. Survival was my constant way of life.

Running off into the sunset with a few of the men who shone their egos on me for more than a few hours never was my fantasy. Yes, I would have preferred to be married to the man with whom I shared a house in Montpelier, Vermont. I didn't dream of becoming his wife, even though I confess to a wee disappointment that a gown I envisaged wearing for the wedding ceremony, a gown hued to the delicacy of a Vermont sunset, never appeared in my closet. The sunsets over the Chateauguay wilderness behind the Fan House are as close as I come to being embraced by coral. Black is the dominant color in my wardrobe.

Scratching the surface of "having a dream" is just like buying lottery tickets. Both unearth a world of fantasy. Both lead to disappointments; one, maybe both, costs money. At the end, dreams are diversionary tactics.

But once this realist did harbor a dream. My three brothers and I owned twenty-seven acres in the south of Oregon's Willamette Valley. We held back this acreage when the rest of what had constituted our legacy, Duncan & Sons Dairy, was sold after our parents died. The acreage is much as it was when I was growing up there in the 1940s and 1950s. While never prosperous, the Unity community between Lowell and Fall Creek now shows signs of transience and decay. Meadows once flourishing with alfalfa and fields staked with green beans bound for the local cannery are fallow and overgrown. Oak trees are weighed down with moss that was nonexistent when our family moved to the Willamette Valley in 1945. But between then and now is a fair amount of time for mosses to congregate on trees and wooden shakes on barn roofs to rot.

Those twenty-seven acres and the nearby fallow fields are under an hour's drive from Oregon wineries, set pieces for how vision had the power to transform landscapes, communities and economies.

Here's how I saw the dream evolving. Some of the acreage we owned was doubtless suited to growing vines. Imagine a vineyard hugging the creek bank just there, at the historical treasure known as the Unity Covered Bridge. While we had limited space to grow vines, we could create a best-practices vineyard that would be a pioneering model for how to create similar projects on nearby fallow land. Within a few years we would be supplying our harvest to regional vintners. Other local landowners could well be pursued by vintners seeking new sources of grapes, and subsequently supported in efforts to plant vines.

This was not a pipe dream. In my mind, it was a given that the vineyard could become a reality. I was willing to put my own limited savings on the table to make this happen. But there was one stumbling block. The land was for sale at the time. My brothers' wives wanted nothing to do with vineyards. Even though my brothers and I all were attached to this land, cashing out by selling was the unstated but preferred alternative to creating a vineyard that would require us all to agree if the project were to fly. Some years later, when the land was still on the market, we passed up one opportunity, in deference to our parents whose ashes are scattered here, to sell to someone who had a dream of growing medical marijuana. Enough already. This would be tantamount to stomping on our parents' resting place. On the farm acres that we had already sold, the owners were using the milking parlor as a workshop for creating marijuana pipes.

Eric Asimov in September 2016 wrote in *The New York Times*: "Many other wine regions around the world have staked their claims as suitable homes for pinot noir. Not all have been consistently successful, but the Willamette Valley of Oregon, in its roughly 50-year history as a wine region, has proved to be one of the best."

I lacked sufficient capital to buy out my brothers and pursue the vineyard project. I'll go to my grave not knowing if our grapes would have produced a decent pinot noir.

On Becoming

In the process of becoming, I say to you,
are you in a state of becoming too?

Impostor Syndrome

We don't know we've always been shadows until we realize that one day we'll be only the shadows we leave behind. And thus begins the process of laying one shadow on top of another on top of another. We all want to write our own obituaries, right?

These days I work hard to control my environment. I keep my desk tidy. Make my bed. Meet deadlines without procrastinating. But sometimes tidy just isn't possible.

Daughter drops off Yorkie puppy for me to babysit while she's in New York. Puppy (of a breed called Teacup Yorkie for its diminutive size of four to seven pounds) is not yet reliably house-trained. I have many carpets. Ergo, the puppy spends the day on a leash tethered along to the porch rail, as does my big white dog.

I plan early dinner. Turn on stove to heat up pasta with delicious homemade pesto and asparagus. Fall asleep on the porch couch. Do not hear fire alarms throughout my house. Neighbors rush over because they hear the alarms. Frantic efforts to rid the house of smoke before bed-and-breakfast guests (full house) return are futile. I can only rely on their kindness. While kitchen door is open to air out house, bird nesting in corner of porch flies into house. Guests note this. I shoo bird out, I think. Collapse into bed, nostrils full of burnt dinner and tummy empty. No dinner for Sara tonight. Puppy is on bed with me. By 4 a.m. I am trying to keep him quiet. He has a nasty little bark.

Get up early. Re-tether both dogs to front porch. I start breakfast for guests. Bird that I thought had left last night swoops through dining room. Now it's out. Count cars in drive. Should be three plus mine; only two plus mine. Did one of my guests seek shelter elsewhere, where there's no smell of burnt food? Note black car with lights on in neighbor's drive. Don't think much about it. Late-arriving guest parked in neighbor's driveway because there was no room to park at the inn, or so guest perceived. I suggest guest get her keys and move the car before the neighbor is up. Car battery dead. I try to help by calling her car insurance company but can't get past the prompts because they want a cell phone number. This I can't provide because we don't have cell service in Barnard. Waiting until 8 a.m. so I can call local car repair that also tows. Can't wait to know what the next chapter is! Have a lovely day.

Local car repair shop owner appears with battery cables to start my guest's car, which is in my neighbor's driveway. Low-budget rental car refuses to start. The only thing percolating is the car alarm that goes off forever, repeatedly. Terse email arrives from neighbor: "Please tell your guests not to park in our driveway." Car finally starts. My attempted joke with owner of the repair shop, a man about my age, falls short when I quip: "Well, we used to have life in the fast lane; now we're in the last lane." I find bird droppings on the living room lampshade and elsewhere. The culprit is a kingbird, a member of the tyrant flycatcher family. Probably good to have around as they keep the black fly and mosquito populations under control on my porch.

Day progresses, and I fulfill a guest's request that I gather lilacs for her room. Since my lilacs are mostly gone, it was literally a stretch to get to some top branches still blooming on one of the bushes. Guest and the others, who also received lilacs so they didn't feel slighted, are pleased. Evening repairs into night, or my early-to-bed version. I bring daughter's Yorkie, who has used his wee-wee pad successfully all day, onto my bed because I assume this is where he will not bark in the middle of the night. Puppy resists going to bed and goes airborne not once but twice off my very high bed. He then scrambles under the bed, near the wall, in a space about a foot wide. I leave him pouting there for some minutes before digging down between the bed and wall to get him out, fearing that his exercises in flying might have injured him. My efforts to retrieve puppy are successful; he's unharmed. But carrying the senior hips that I do, I was almost wedged into the space between wall and bed. Had good fortune not smiled on me, I would have had to prevail on the guests chattering in the living room some yards away. However, a cry for help is not required. Puppy is then relegated overnight to my office, and the day ends on a singularly peaceful note.

Vestal virgins deserve adjectives like "vulnerable" and "gullible." Women should run as fast as they can away from these traits that too often become putty in the hands of perceived authority figures and borderline sociopaths. I didn't know about needing to run until damage was done. In retrospect, perhaps the damage began when I was an impressionable young child, integrating into an impressionable psyche the lyrics from a Victor Herbert operetta. The song is called *Always Do as People Say You Should*:

> *Always do as people say you should*
> *You never can be happy child unless you're good …*
> *I was so good.*

A documentary released in 2022, *Keep Sweet: Pray and Obey*, reveals a cult mentality that threatened to destroy psyches and indeed lives.

Although this was not my family's cult, they laid expectations on me that were eerily similar.

I must forgive myself, forgive others and simply accept fate.

Transformation

On the near side of childhood I picked up a book.
I know just where I was when I first took a look
at the small orange book from my Mother's case
that I proceeded to read at a feverish pace
while tucked in a tiny room overlooking the field,
my Story Book dolls a decorative shield
of bonnets and satins on a shelf o'er the bed,
those notions of frothy romances that fled
as Lysistrata grabbed a place in my mind
with a power too strong for my young head to find
but one that came with me with dolls packed away,
a power that seeped into both work and play —
the notion that women can chart their own course,
can be what they choose — an impregnable force.
Thank you, Dear Friends, for helping this voice
recall that at all times we girls have a choice
to be butterflies pinioned in dusty frames
or soaring wings spread with our own names
emblazoned on strifes and successes,
as free as our men to mop up our messes.
But when, Dear Ladies, can we ever see
that we will ever be truly, historically free
of the myths of those story books read as a child
that tempered us girls to be always mild
while waiting for any Tom, Dick or Harry
to wander our way so we might marry?

In the Beginning

Ripples in a stream never replicate themselves. A snapshot here; a vignette there. A ripple from the past, but never the same ripple. Think of life lived in the glare of a strobe light. A snapshot here, a vignette there. The effect is akin to French writer Chateaubriand's observation that we have not one life, but many lives laid end to end.

In the thrall of moving currents, the *I* in that snapshot, the *I* in that vignette once lived. Memories emerge. Time cuts the fog. Today I decide what to dig up and how the memories will be recast. But first I have to dig deep. Why was I there? Who was I then? I ask myself to witness the same accident and report on its aftermath. My reports vary. Does this mean that a recalled experience can never be true? Perhaps.

Now, these years later, in the process of coming to grips with my story, I flash in and out and in and out, as if in the thrall of a strobe light.

"Things fall apart ... the centre cannot hold," Yeats predicted.

I traveled because I could, in great part thanks to clients who required that I sit at their tables, sleep in their five-star hotel beds, ride on their trains and boats, and explore this oh-so-fragile world in places as far flung as Australia's Great Barrier Reef, Burma, Istanbul and Botswana. Other journeys that I took were mine to sort out. Three personal expeditions were excuses to ignore problems and to defer decisions. For three weeks I ran to the former Soviet Union to get away from a lover. For another three weeks I ran to India to escape the isolation and cold of a New Hampshire ski resort. I ran to China for six weeks to escape the reality that the company I had founded had fallen apart.

These personal journeys precipitated change. They presaged boxes and U-Hauls, despair, detritus and departures; but departures to where, I never fully understood.

What I did know was that somewhere between conceiving and birthing my second child, life as I knew it went off the rails. Between then and now, however, I've had experiences that would make a sybarite drool, including riding the rails on more than one occasion in a style known to those familiar with Agatha Christie's *Murder on the Orient Express.*

Does this mean I never got my life back on track? You decide, after you have watched me chasing shadows, dancing in the strobe light.

Coloring Life

Don't come to me for subtle
'cause everything's intense.
Seek ye not for pastels
or it's at your own expense.

Chronology

1960 Married at twenty; moved from Lowell, Oregon, to Italy and Germany with husband serving as lieutenant in the Signal Corps for the United States Army

1963 Returned from Europe to study at Stanford; received undergraduate degree in English literature with a minor in journalism

1965 Gave birth to first daughter while living in Portland, Oregon

1965 Worked toward an advanced degree in American literature; taught English and journalism at brand-new high school

1967 Pregnant with second child; husband diagnosed with manic-depressive disorder; played ping-pong with sick husband in the hospital's psychiatric ward

1968 Second daughter born; husband (under treatment) resigned job with major educational broadcasting organization in Portland to assume fundraising position with a public broadcasting network in New York; family moved to Brooklyn Heights, New York

1970 Moved from cramped apartment in Brooklyn Heights to a small bungalow on Staten Island; husband struggling with mental illness and now with alcohol misuse, a combination that terminated his public television career

1972 Purchased country store in East Poultney, Vermont; husband began series of peregrinations, ultimately deserting family

1975 To support family (no child support forthcoming), I became news bureau director at a major ski resort in New England; divorced at thirty-five

1980 Resigned ski resort post; took position as reporter on city desk with United Press International in New York City; worked for Hawk Public Relations

1981   Affair of heart prompted move with two daughters to
       Montpelier, Vermont; served as lifestyle and business editor
       for *Montpelier-Barre Times-Argus*; also did freelance writing
       and served as public relations director for another Vermont
       ski resort; resigned newspaper position to become marketing
       director of condominium development project perched on a
       mountainside in central Vermont; live-in partner (affair of the
       heart) left

1986   Moved to New Hampshire to become marketing director for a
       four-season resort

1988   Moved to New York City; began working for public relations
       firms, specializing in travel and lifestyle

1990s Created Sara Widness Communications, which later morphed
       into another entity when I invited a partner to join me

1998   Purchased the Fan House in Barnard, Vermont; began
       renovating this 1840 heirloom that eventually would serve as
       bed-and-breakfast accommodation

2001   Airplanes flew into World Trade Center on 9/11; businesses in
       travel sector lost clients; company tightened belt but there were
       no layoffs

2002   Palace coup early in year savaged the public relations company
       that I had so carefully nurtured and that was reeling from 9/11
       impact; closed New York office and moved to Vermont full-time

2003   Received license to open the Fan House Bed and Breakfast;
       began consultancy Widness & Wiggins Public Relations, with
       focus on international adventure; began writing freelance stories
       for local newspapers and magazines

2020   Covid-19 pandemic forced shuttering of both bed and breakfast
       and public relations consultancy

2021   Re-opened bed and breakfast in May

From the Algarve

How can we know that toddler hands
placing jigsawed pieces of a bird or goat
will later search chips of blue and yellow bands
from a Portuguese bowl,
fractured flowers dropped to be glued in place
to embrace these oranges weighing down tree-filled groves
glimpsed through rain between the Algarve cliffs,
those high places where whitewashed houses splinter sometimes
on the sand when the sea furls?

The Awakening

Our Volkswagen was stuffed with my sewing machine and the rest of our earthly goods. Waving goodbye to friends and family, our "I do's" still ringing in the air, my husband and I drove away from the church in Eugene, Oregon, and headed off on a cross-country adventure that would lead to a steamy summer in Long Branch, New Jersey. My husband was a second lieutenant in the United States Army Signal Corps. He was assigned to Fort Monmouth, New Jersey. This was a temporary assignment. In a few months we would sail across the Atlantic. Waiting to embrace us, compliments of the United States Army, were Italy and a two-year tour of duty in Tuscany, followed by a one-year tour of duty in Germany.

Other than photos of the wedding and reception, I don't have mementos of our leave-taking. I had changed into a sheath that I had created from green *peau de soie*. I wore these with matching shoes, a pillbox hat and white gloves. For a few hours before, however, I had become the princess in the wedding gown of embroidered silk organza. This exquisite fabric was personally chosen for my gown by the proprietor of a fabric store in Eugene, Oregon. I designed the gown and left it to the kindness of a neighbor, a talented seamstress, to create the floor-length fantasy with tiny bound buttons up the back and a twenty-three-inch waist.

A few hours later my husband and I were seated at a restaurant on the McKenzie River. We tried to feign worldliness as we forked freshly caught trout into our mouths. Any intimations of sophisticate collapsed, however, when at the end of the meal I stood up. All of the rice that was showered on us as we left the church had collected atop my strapless bustier (called a "merry widow"). I left a pool of rice under my chair and dribbled a trail out to the cabin, where my husband was eager to engage with my virginity. He deferred this activity for a few days. I was embarrassed that my period had started the morning we said our vows.

Adventures came our way as we headed east out of Oregon. We skinny-dipped in a river in northern Idaho before bunking down one night in Lemmon, North Dakota, in a motel that was undergoing restoration. A large plastic sheet separated our room from the next. Fortunately, nobody was in the other room. By the time we reached Minnesota our yellow Volkswagen "bug" was no longer bright and shiny. When we stopped for gas, the gas station owner voluntarily hosed down the car.

Unbeknownst to me, the bridegroom had left Oregon with his new bride and only what remained of his monthly military paycheck in his pocket. How much this was, I never knew. But he advised midway on our journey that what he had in his wallet would have to get us through from July 9, the day we were married, until early August, when he was paid again. The concept of scrimping was new to me. Although my family was far from wealthy, as children and now as young adults, my brothers and I never wanted for anything. If my parents ever worried about resources, we never knew about it. We pulled our weight on the farm and were compensated.

Suddenly I was anxious. As newlyweds we had been gifted by friends and family. Friends gave us a ceramic plate for deviled eggs, a silver nut dish, sterling forks and spoons, the writings of Kahlil Gibran, a lace tablecloth and the list goes on. My parents gave us the new Singer sewing machine and to me a three-piece suite of cream-colored Samsonite luggage, compliments of Green Stamps they'd hoarded for months. Somehow the idea of money in my pocket had been overlooked. Just how far would somewhere around $200 go?

We unpacked the car some days later in Long Branch, New Jersey. For the next two months we snuggled into a two-room (kitchen and bedroom) apartment on the second floor of a private home owned by a suspicious Italian landlady. The only phone we had access to was on the landing outside our door. We weren't her only tenants. Someone was abusing the phone privileges and making long-distance calls. She put a lock on the phone. The sidewalk to the front door was guarded by an equally suspicious dog, a Chow Chow. This creature protected her house with vigorous barking and bared teeth that never failed to set my heart racing.

By the end of July we were down to half-dollars. My penchant to show off 4-H trained culinary talents were put on hold, as ingredients for the elaborate cakes and main courses I longed to make were too pricey for our budget. As we slipped in and out of our newlywed bed, time slipped into August and the next payday. I didn't know it at the time, but new seeds were being sewn. I had a growing anathema to any kind of dependency that affected financial stability and well-being. This anathema would eventually play out as a take-charge, do-it-myself independence and a distrust of any kind of authority or paternalism that made me in any way dependent, financially or otherwise.

I think I breathed deeply for the first time since our wedding day when weeks later we overnighted in officers' quarters at the United States Army Garrison Fort Hamilton in Brooklyn, New York, prior to boarding the ship that would carry us across the Atlantic Ocean to our new life.

Our first taste of *il bel Paese* came with the formally attired Italian waiters who served our equally formal table on the *USNS General Maurice Rose*. The ship was in service from 1950 to 1967 and scrapped in 2000. In 1957 her voyages included transporting refugees from Hungary to the United States. Three years later, in October 1960, we were enjoying first-class service along with the company of a charming officer of the Turkish air force who taught us how to say "thank you" in his language. Also on board was a worldly young couple from Venezuela, perhaps enjoying the fruits of that country's then burgeoning petroleum industry. Although I was too naïve at the time to understand why, this blonde twosome exuded the confidence of the very rich.

The ship's most traveled route was between New York and Bremerhaven, Germany, but she also traveled to the Mediterranean. Her first stop on our journey was for refueling at what is now NAVSTA Rota, the largest American military base in Spain. A next brief stop was Barcelona, Spain. Our final stop was Livorno, Italy. In Rota we briefly disembarked. To our horror, as we walked through the town we witnessed village youth throwing stones at a mentally handicapped man. After this encounter with this medieval behavior, flamenco music and dancers lured us into a nightclub in Barcelona. When we reached Livorno, our final destination, a variation on medieval spikes reminded us that we were no longer in Kansas. Shards of glass were embedded in cement on the tops of concrete walls near where the ship was docked.

As in the decades leading up to the early 1960s, Americans who traveled to Europe or anywhere in the world that was exotic represented the wealthy who enjoyed such perceived privileges as mingling for "the season" on the French Riviera or dressing for dinner and a night at the casino in Monte Carlo. The idea that young people like us could expand their horizons by traveling abroad wasn't yet common. The Peace Corps began expanding minds when it sprang to life in 1961, a year after our military-sponsored adventure began.

For the next two years we would live first on the second floor of a tile-roofed stucco villa with marble floors that was across a thorough-fare from the Tyrrhenian (Ligurian) Sea. Our second home was on the ground floor of a similarly appointed villa tucked a few blocks away in a grove of pine trees. Both houses were in Tirrenia, a resort town in central Tuscany, at the southern end of the Italian Riviera, just minutes from Darby Military Community, USAG Italy, which we knew as Camp Darby.

According to the U.S. Department of Defense, "In June 1951, the United States and Italy concluded negotiations to establish a line of communication and supply through Italy, in support of U.S. troops stationed in Austria." That installation, which is a ten-minute drive from Pisa and an hour by train or car from Florence, became a permanent facility in 1952.

My Second Lieutenant husband assumed duties at Camp Darby for two years. I unpacked my sewing machine and cookbooks and poured myself into domesticity. Our furnished villas were part of a network of homes rented to military personnel because Camp Darby did not have sufficient housing. This system, called "living on the economy," required the government to provide a monthly housing stipend. The reason we moved from one villa to the next had to do with economics. The second house, back in the pine forest, was cheaper than the villa on the sea. The stipend stayed the same and we could save a few dollars each month for our travel account. We also saved money by not hiring household help. Having a domestic servant was the norm for officers and their families. But we preferred to travel. Our parsimony did lead to one near-disaster. I decided to clean the marble floors in our first villa. The only way I knew how to clean floors was to get down on my knees with a bucket of water and a cloth and start scrubbing. This was followed by a good waxing. My knees were blistered for weeks and the apartment was a skating rink, lethal but glowing.

Tirrenia, known as "The Pearl of the Mediterranean Sea," was birthed from the marshes by Benito Mussolini in World War II. His vision for the Italian fascist party that he founded in 1919 extended to creating a film capital here, as well as homes for orphaned children and dwellings for the wealthy. Certainly this was a bravura gesture appealing to the then-fascist sentiments.

Although it would be nice to remember Sara venturing from the new-lywed's villa into this small town to select fresh fruits and vegetables for our dinners, I was *una straniera* and intimidated. I had two years of high school Spanish and two years of college French, neither of which served me in figuring out how much lira I would need for a transaction. The military base provided well-stocked shelves of groceries and collectibles from all over the world that we could access with a military discount.

The region was once the home of the Etruscans, an ancient people with an unsurpassed *joie de vivre*. This just-post World War II Italy retained war memories, still raw from hunger. We stumbled on one of these memories on a Sunday afternoon. Somewhere near Livorno, in a drab, concrete building on a hill with a view of the sea, were plaques to the memory of Mussolini's daughter, Edda Ciano, and her husband, Count Galeazzo Ciano, who was Mussolini's propaganda czar and who died by execution. Only decades later after stories of World War II were aired in print and then in movie houses and on television did I begin to com-prehend the tragedy of the Nazi occupation of Italy. Not enough time had passed by 1960, fifteen years after the war ended, to fill in the bullet holes scarring so many buildings nor to rebuild a trust between us, the *stranieri*, and some of the people we passed on the sidewalks, and some of the shop keepers and waiters who may have greeted us with coolness.

Under the pines in the garden surrounding our villa, our landlord, who doubtless had experienced hunger pangs during the war, shot *uccel-li* (sparrows) that he roasted on a spit. We were horrified by this practice until we dined at a restaurant in Torre del Lago, where Puccini once lived. There, not far from Viareggio, Ristorante Da Cecco had an open fire in a large hearth over which skewered *uccelli* sizzled. What once seemed bar-baric was now fine dining. However, we opted instead for *cinghiale* (wild boar), preceded by a *crostini* I've never been able to replicate.

Even though the sea lapped at our doorstep, on weekends we pre-ferred dashing by car into hilltop villages. Our transportation was an

Austin-Healy Sprite, an English sports car and our flying carpet across Italy and much of Europe. In near-deserted villages the locals sometimes asked if we knew their relatives in Chicago. World War II and one-way, trans-Atlantic crossings had taken their toll. Even today communities throughout Italy are up for grabs as young people leave for the cities. Unlike today's manicured Tuscan hilltop towns, filled with boutiques and galleries and visitors, those same towns in 1960 were drab and gray. Women wore mostly black; both the elderly and the young were in mourning for lost sons and husbands. On Sundays the palette livened up during the traditional weekly stroll, the *passeggiata*. Often *vechiette* (old women wearing black) demonstrated how war had ravaged them. Beneath their skirts were thin, bowed legs that testified to rickets, a condition of the bones brought on by a vitamin D deficiency they suffered while growing up. Blue jeans were still years away. Men always wore wool jackets over dark wool trousers held up with a belt. Even lines of laundry strung across narrow streets lacked color. Back then, few potted geraniums graced the doorsteps. Signs encouraging people to "Vota Communista" were common. Children would rush to our car, a curiosity to them, in hopes we would give them candy. But on chilly winter days, we were wary of welcomes we might receive from men clad in dark navy or black trench coats, slouched over cigarettes while strolling by.

On our forays, village churches that were always cold lured us out of the sun, sometimes into explosions of color created by mosaics surrounding a simple altar. Wrapped in the memory of these rainbows, we would then settle down to yet another lunch at a *trattoria*. For two years we ate enough pasta to move one of us in the direction of becoming *un po ingrassata* (a little chubby).

However, I had an antidote to this tendency to plump. Early in college, I went to a doctor in Oregon. I weighed in at around 120 pounds then. Unasked, he prescribed diet pills to decrease my appetite. Was this a way to curb my enthusiasm or did he just prefer skinny girls? I took his pills — amphetamine or speed — without question. They did the job. I didn't take them all the time, just when a grand meal was pending or, strangely, if we were going to party. Opening the capsule and sprinkling half of the little colored beads in my hand before the evening began assured me a jolly time. Only when I learned that these pills were killing women in Oregon did I stop taking them. Some years later I substituted running for speed, lapping up highs on my five-mile daily runs. Who was that doctor? Doubtless he was among thousands who were pocketing gifts from pharmaceutical profits. The opioid pandemic raging in the first decades of the 21st century may be analogous to the speed epidemic in the mid-20th century.

For two years my husband and I played our hearts out (mine with extra help from speed) as we imbibed the beauty of frescoed, painted and mosaicked Madonnas and embraced the magnificence of live opera. At Maggio Musicale in Florence we heard Renata Tebaldi perform the role of a doomed heroine. Hers was the first of many voices I now cherish. We never fell short of being appreciative audience members. We picnicked by rivers, skied in the Apennine Mountains, learned to enjoy wines, played the slot machines at the Officers' Club, drove weekly to Livorno for Italian lessons and purchased alabaster fruit from the marble world of Carrara. We witnessed the spectacle of *Carnevale* in Via Reggio, a town on the Gulf of La Spezia where Percy Bysshe Shelley drowned.

We thirsted for excitement, paying for it on a cramped military salary that I supplemented by teaching remedial courses to soldiers who needed to obtain their General Educational Development (GED) certificates in order to achieve a promotion. I was paid $5 per class. Weekdays I took a short bus ride from Tirrenia to the military base to receive my instructions from the education director for whom I worked, Ted Jacobs.

Ted had a live-in companion who may have been his wife. I never met her. He said on her arm were numbers tattooed while she was a prisoner in a concentration camp. Photographs in *Life* had introduced me as a young girl to the concept of numbers tattooed onto an arm. But I don't think the horrors of the Holocaust had yet entered my psyche. Perhaps Ted Jacobs was in my young life to wake me up.

The Camp Darby campus where I taught is tucked into a grove of pines indigenous to that part of the Tyrrhenian coast. Stories still echoed of the World War II battles waged in the nearby Tombolo Woods by a contingent of Black soldiers serving in the United States Army. Walking under the pine trees around the military base made the World War II stories more real. Today the pines of the Tomboli di Cecina Nature Reserve buffer land from sea.

Another man who worked at the education center became a close friend. He, his wife, my husband and I made an inseparable foursome, laughing when the tire rolled off their car as we were riding to Pisa and commiserating when one of us sprained an ankle skiing at Abetone, a ski resort in the Italian Apennine Mountains. At the base theater, three of us took on roles in *The Glass Menagerie*. Two of us squared off in *The Unicorn in the Garden*. Each script presaged later events in my marriage. The play by Tennessee Williams showered me with premonitions of loss and longing. The Thurber fable dogged my husband and me. A man spots this white beast, the unicorn, in his garden, only to be reminded by his wife of the difference between make-believe and reality.

Wild Rose

Wafts of wild rose glance over the lake
between splays of yellow flag
stalking like herons near the bank
and the dance the sun displays
out where the water's deep.

Ciao, Bella

When orders came for a transfer from Italy to Germany, we sold the Sprite that had squired us through Italy's sunshine. Farther north we didn't see the sun for days on end in winter. Again we opted to live in a village house "on the economy" and located an apartment on the second floor of a private home in Edingen, located between the university town of Heidelberg, which had escaped war's wrath, and the heavily bombed, industrial city of Mannheim.

The open foyer at the top of the stairs became our de facto living room. To the right was a bedroom and on the other side was the kitchen. A second room, off limits to us, was used as a study by the landlord's daughter. We felt uncomfortable in our "living room" when Anneliese was next door. Any hot water available to the apartment was heated by a gas unit fixed over the bathtub and fired up at will. We carried hot water from there through the "living room" to the kitchen.

If a horse sauntered by on the cobblestone street, our landlord would dash out to collect manure for his garden. In spring his wife left bowls of fresh strawberries or parcels of white asparagus at our door. Wafting scents of *rouladen*, a staple of this *hausfrau's* weekend kitchen, always reminded us which day was Sunday.

Shopping in Edingen in 1962 required fortitude. Seventeen years ago, in 1945, the United States had helped in Germany's defeat in World War II. Memories were raw. Some German men at that time disliked having Americans in their village. Several times I was forced off the sidewalk and into the gutter by a still-angry man. (This get-off-my-sidewalk syndrome was expressed in the early 1970s in Manhattan. I experienced such aggression from some very angry men at a time when the Black Panthers were making a name for themselves.)

Just after our arrival in Germany, the Cuban missile crisis pulsed from October 16 to October 28, 1962. This contretemps followed the erection of the Berlin Wall on August 12 and 13, 1961. The Communist authorities of the German Democratic Republic, with the encouragement of the Soviet Union's front man, Nikita Khrushchev, hoped to halt an east-to-west migration of a war-ravaged population that preferred to live in Berlin's French, English and American zones instead of the Russian zone. From 1945 to 1961 an estimated 3 to 3.5 million people left East Berlin.

The Wall would stay put for the next thirty-seven years, a reminder of the ugliness of the Cold War that was waged until it came down on November 9, 1989.

The October crisis involving the Republic of Cuba was a stand-off between the United States and the Communist Soviet Union. At issue, in part, was an American deployment of ballistic missiles to Italy and Turkey. This was threatening to the Soviet Union, which countered with a similar deployment of ballistic missiles to its friend, Cuba, ninety miles from Florida. The players were President John F. Kennedy, Cuba's Prime Minister Fidel Castro and Khrushchev. Military personnel on the United States Army military base in Mannheim (six hours by car from Berlin and a short commute from Edingen, where we lived) were on high alert and working overtime during this crisis. This included my first lieutenant husband, whose work as a crypto specialist was top secret.

In military terms he held what was known as top-secret "crypto clearance." Crypto is short for cryptography, the process of writing or deciphering messages in code. Long before the days of cyberspace, his crypto assignment at Camp Darby in Italy was to transmit messages via a secure, world-wide, long-distance radio transmission network called STARCOM (Strategic Army Communications). In the 21st Signal Company at Camp Darby, he was alternately the supply officer, radio officer and communication center officer. In Mannheim he was assigned to the U.S. Seventh Army Infantry Maintenance Group (IMG). Part of his IMG mission put him in charge of storing and maintaining tactical cryptographic equipment for the U.S. Army's 4th Infantry Division. That division supported U.S. forces in West Berlin. The whole strategic deployment was called "Operation Long Thrust."

Over Christmas 1961, before we moved from Italy to Germany, we were guests of a German friend and his parents in Berlin. The Berlin Wall had gone up in August 1961. During this Christmas in Berlin we watched the promenade on the west side of the Berlin Wall. Passers-by often tossed packages of cigarettes up to the East German soldiers assigned by the German Democratic Republic to patrol the perimeter from the top of the Wall. The River Spree, now frozen, paralleled part of *die Mauer* (the wall). On a light post hung a photo of one of the eighty people who died trying to exit East Berlin, doubtless shot while crossing the river by one of those soldiers up there marching back and forth. Below a photograph of his body was written: *Du könntest unser Bruder sein.* This means: You could be our brother.

Our host's father had high-level agricultural connections in what was then East Germany. He had met his wife-to-be while managing her father's estate on the other side of the Wall. Now he worried about the people he knew and how he could get care packages to them.

On this visit our host took us to the main gate that allowed authorized traffic between East and West Berlin. This was Checkpoint Charlie. Christian Bonte-Friedheim, our host, laughed as I squawked in the back seat when he drove us into East Berlin and briefly toward Potsdam, an act that was *verboten* to American military personnel with a crypto clearance. Chris was playing a dangerous game with us.

Because my husband had crypto clearance, we could not travel by automobile in or out of Berlin, let alone be found wandering on the wrong side of the divided city. To reach Berlin we'd taken a military train there from Frankfurt, fearful as East German soldiers checked our passports at the border between East Berlin and one of the three western zones. Christian invited us to spend a week with him sampling wines along the Mosel. He drove his car out of the city. Because of the top-secret clearance that my military mate held, we could not drive out of the city. We flew from Berlin to Düsseldorf to meet him. Here we toured his uncle's factory, which manufactured fire extinguishers.

Now we were again in Germany, almost a year later. During the Cuban stand-off, we had no television in our village apartment. Radio reports in English were hard to come by. My husband spent nights on the military base in Mannheim. When we were together, he was visibly worried, as was I. Our concerns spanned the globe: We worried for ourselves, sitting ducks in the middle of the European potboiler still simmering and still armed and ready after two world wars; for our country, which might now be easily attacked; for the people of Cuba who would disappear in any American counterattack; and for our families, who were supposedly out of harm's way on the West Coast — but were they? After that crisis the world could breathe deeply again. In that same troubled year, the Moscow–Washington hotline was established to help cool leaders off before they started sweating. We could now hope that the chief of the free world and that of the not-so-free Union of Soviet Socialist Republics (USSR) would always have enough self-discipline to use this line before egos prevailed.

Weekdays when I boarded the bus that took me from Edingen to Heidelberg, a woman motioned me to sit with her. I think she was practicing her English. Our conversation was about her passion for going to the woods on weekends in search of *Pilz* (mushrooms) and *Erholung* (rest and relaxation). Another kind of rest and relaxation occurred every morning around ten in the office where I worked at the University of Maryland in Heidelberg. My colleagues unwrapped pungent, meat-filled sandwiches for their leisurely *Frühstück* (a late brunch or an early lunch). My job there was to compose and type on an old-fashioned typewriter responses to soldiers who were behind on tuition payments for the courses they were taking through the university. My letters, however, often missed the mark when I consoled the soldiers for misfortunes they revealed in their correspondence, misfortunes that had brought them to this sad pecuniary state. The director of this division, an American, and his fashionista assistant from Latvia smirked while pointing out my errors.

Once again we were also students, taking lessons in German at the University of Maryland. Weekends found us strolling Philosophenweg, a trail leading up a steep hill to a view of Heidelberg. One Sunday while sitting on a bench on this trail, I, still a new bride, shared my darkest, most shameful secret with my husband. I told him that just before I turned thirteen, a boy who lived across the road from my family's farm stalked me to the riverbank on my parents' property. He carried a hunting rifle that he pointed at me as he commanded me to take off all my clothes by the count of ten . . . or else. I did, he didn't and I ran sobbing back to the farmhouse.

After this revelation in the wilderness and *frische Luft* (fresh air), we commiserated over hot chocolate and *Gebäck* (pastry) at the café that concluded our climb. Heidelberg was my fairy-tale city. While growing up one of my favorite operettas was *The Student Prince*. I longed to hear refrains of "Drink! Drink! Drink! To eyes that are bright as stars when they're shining on me!" In Old Heidelberg we were introduced to *Rotkohl* (red cabbage) at the Student Prince Café.

Before We Knew

So much we did not know
but knew before we knew each other
that knowing is rain on apple blossoms,
the tracery of snow around the field,
a violin concerto fraught with surprise.
As knowing chases memories,
we did not know but knew
knowing would be all of risks and more.

Halcyon Days

Career military personnel were gearing up for Vietnam in 1964. This family's tour of duty was over. The Army packed us up and flew us from Germany home to the United States. We had consumed as much of Europe as we had time and money for. Stanford University was the next stop. The region that in 1971 would be dubbed Silicon Valley included Palo Alto, California, the university's hometown. While studying for an advanced degree in communications, my husband worked as a reporter for the *Sunnyvale Standard*, published in the neighboring town of Sunnyvale.

We only planned to be at Stanford for nine months, the time required for one of us to earn his advanced degree. My goal was to earn an undergraduate degree during this time. This would be possible if I acquired as many course credits as was humanly possible each semester. As a result I accomplished in one year what should have been two years of undergraduate studies in English literature. In part this was thanks to two years of undergraduate studies accomplished before I was married, plus extra language credits the university awarded me for some knowledge of German and Italian, and thanks to credits for mail-order semesters of Victorian literature that the University of Oregon had mailed to me in Italy.

I was taking so many classes that time out to spend a few hours with friends was out of the question for me. Resentment crept in, however, the weekend we were invited to a West Coast equivalent of a Grand Prix. I misinterpreted an assignment on Edmund Spenser's *The Faerie Queene* and thought I was to read the whole book over the weekend, instead of just a few chapters. We had loved every minute of the theater of a European Grand Prix a year or so ago. I was now confined to the built-in desk in our Menlo Park apartment, disliking Spenser more every minute.

Vestiges of a military presence in Menlo Park, a five-minute drive to

Stanford University, included a string of one-story barracks now devoted to student housing. I don't know what housing accommodations were like for students who lived on campus in 1964. I'm sure other students in this enclave of red-tile roofs and manicured Mission Revival elegance that is Stanford were more comfortably sheltered than we were.

Compliments of the United States Army, a moving van delivered our worldly possessions to our Menlo Park door. This was the next-to-last time someone else footed the bill for packing up and moving our Duncan Phyfe dining table and chairs, this suite of furniture being the only large thing we sent home from Germany. Souvenirs, dishes, linens and clothes filled the stack of boxes inside the dark living room of this barracks apartment. In addition to the living room with the built-in desk where I studied were a bedroom, kitchen and bathroom.

Among our neighbors was a couple who celebrated Ramadan, something neither of us had heard of until they broke their fast. Our contiguous walls were paper thin and we were inadvertently involved in their celebrations.

Because I appropriated the only exterior wall for studying and typing papers, the other student in the household was left with the bathroom. He sat here so the sound of the typewriter would not disturb our neighbors.

Spenser may have played a part in my decision at this time not to pursue a doctoral degree. Most certainly Milton did. While roving the heavens with Milton's angels I was dissuaded from moving into the highest academic spheres. Other than Milton, however, I cherished every book I was privileged to read and every lecture I was privileged to attend for my courses. The lectures were pure theater to me, dramas in which professors minute by minute compelled me to enter their wise and erudite lairs. I lived in the library stacks, compelled hour after hour to find the magical keys that would transform my understanding of an author or an issue, only to realize as I sorted through cards of handwritten notes and quotes that it was I who held the magic key and who could create new understandings of decades- and centuries-old studies. With particular pride I remember a highest mark on a paper on William Golding's *Lord of the Flies*. The professor wrote that this was the best explication of the book that he had ever read. Over a four-hour history exam we were to write in response to two questions. I became so absorbed in the first question that there was no time left for the second. When I handed my blue book (the book in which we wrote our exams) to the professor I told him that question two was not included. Given this omission I received a B+, probably because he recognized I had been seduced by ideas, and isn't that the goal of a university anyway?

I chose a course in logic for the math credits I needed to graduate. Professor Patrick Suppes, who wore a red vest as he lectured, brought me to my knees after each lecture. Bewildered after each class, I begged his teaching assistant to explain what I had just heard, including the professor's references to quadratic equations that I knew nothing about even though, according to him, junior high school students were well versed. After these lectures, the stress and humiliation I carried home bounced off the thin walls of our apartment. The C I received as a logician hung below higher grades at this semester's end.

These intense nine months were followed by another nine-month salvo and the birth of our first daughter in Portland, Oregon. Leaving the San Francisco Bay area behind, we moved north, settling in Portland because my husband accepted a position with the then-fledgling Oregon Public Television. This time we unpacked our worldly goods in a cabin in the woods in southwest Portland, a location so remote that no neighbors' lights shone into our space. When my husband went off to work, I was left with a degree from Stanford and a diminished enthusiasm for domesticity. Plus I was lonely. He tried to assuage my loneliness by gifting me with a wire-haired fox terrier we named Percival, or Percy. He was a sweet addition to our family until struck down on the road near my family's farm while we were visiting.

Bringing a pet into the household is often a harbinger of things to come. In our case Percy presaged the arrival of our first born, whom we brought home not to the cabin in the woods but to an early 20th-century house in southwest Portland that we purchased and were renovating. My water broke while I was vacuuming plaster dust. Our daughter was born in late July 1965.

We were, I think, a happy little family. The only argument I recall during this time was over a new car the head of household parked in front of our house one day. Evidently in his family of origin the husband made all of the big financial decisions. This husband was following suit and didn't tell me he was replacing our admittedly old clunker. But the old clunker was paid for. I was not working. The idea of car payments stirred my anxieties. The new car disappeared. I never gave a thought to how the breadwinner might feel about driving the old clunker to work.

By September of 1966 I was teaching English and supervising the progress of a student newspaper and yearbook at a brand-new high school nearby. We had just the one car. I don't remember how I got back and forth to work. A kind, elderly woman answered our ad for a nanny. She so wanted to take care of all of us that she asked if she could start our dinner preparations before we got home. I went off to the high school with nary a worry. Evenings I took classes at Portland State University that would lead to a Master of Arts in teaching degree.

Or so I hoped.

Purring

I try to recreate my garden in a vase
but butterflies that chase the blossoms
in the sunlight elude this space
with scissors snipping stems once waving,
wafting scents so blurred with color
even the bees purr.

Seven-Year Itch

Seven years almost to the day we were married, a mutation of the seven-year itch moved in with us.

One evening at dinner my husband and I argued about whether he would drive me to my classes in downtown Portland and then pick me up. Keep in mind that I'd learned to drive with little to no traffic, in the countryside. I didn't drive in Europe or while we were at Stanford. I was nervous about driving into the city at any time and especially at night. He was probably thinking about his own mother, who never learned to drive and who always had to depend on his father. He was also concerned, rightfully so, about packing up our two-year-old each time he left the house. He put his foot down and said I would have to drive myself. His decision ended the studies of his by-now newly pregnant wife.

Perhaps this is when I began to realize that things were falling apart. It was the middle of summer in 1967. Only in hindsight can I understand how weighed down this man must have felt. Was he content raising awareness and funds for public television shows? I think so. Was he delighted to be remodeling our house evening after evening and weekend after weekend? He never complained. Was he feeling helpless as he watched his mother sink into the no-way-out destruction caused by ALS, which is also known as Lou Gehrig's Disease? Most certainly. Meanwhile his father, who had long labored to keep his family afloat, was losing his home on the edge of the campus of Oregon State University in Corvallis, Oregon, to eminent domain. The father had just completed a rental unit over his garage, as a hedge against retirement. Did this worry their son? Of course.

One morning he went to the bookshelf in our living room and began loading volumes of the *Great Books of the Western World* series into the car. He said he needed them at his office.

He also began gouging small triangles into the wooden door frames of our home while he was sanding and staining. If I served peas for dinner, he arranged the peas into triangles on his plate.

His conversations seemed to come from worlds far from anything I could begin to understand. He could not sleep. One night around 3 a.m. we went downstairs. To help take his mind off his sleeplessness, I gathered all of the leather shoes in the house and various colors of shoe polish and we polished shoes until it was time for him to shower and go to work.

He still went to work every day and came home for dinner. Bedtime conversations stretched deeper into worlds unknown to me. After nearly a month passed, I realized that what was happening was not going to take care of itself. This poor soul needed to get some sleep. On the premise that he would get help for his sleeplessness, I made arrangements for him to visit the psychiatric ward of the University of Oregon Medical School, located on the campus of Oregon Health and Sciences University in Portland. He, too, must have realized he needed help, as there was no resistance driving from our house up to the hospital.(Since 2007 this medical complex can be accessed from Portland's waterfront by the Portland Aerial Tram, a scenic, 3,300-foot journey.)

In the car he waved his hands on and off the steering wheel. He wanted me to see his wrists, which bore scars from a bout of childhood impetigo. He informed me that these scars were from the time he was nailed to the cross. Any spirit I had left was fast going out the window. When he was checked in at the hospital, he showed the scars to the admitting physician, a Dr. Bishop, and explained to him as well that they were there because he was nailed to the cross. I had to stifle my gasp at the irony of having a man named Bishop attending to this theater. Life had already begun flinging ironies at us, I realized; the director of the television station where my now-agitated friend worked was named Luke Lamb.

After telling about his scars, the man who craved sleep became a resident in the psychiatric ward in November 1967. This stay included a stint in a lockdown cell. For a period of time, evidently, until medications started kicking in, he was out of control.

Our little girl was standing in the doorway between the kitchen and the front hall of our house. She had an apple in her hand and was wearing a cotton dress sprinkled with flowers that I had sewn for her.

"Daddy can't come home," I told her. "Daddy is sick."

After some weeks, the doctors pronounced that my husband had experienced a psychotic break and that he was exhibiting schizoid behavior. The main issue was to determine the mix of pharmaceuticals that would help bring him back to some kind of normalcy. After a few weeks I had visiting rights on the ward. These visits included extended minutes of awkwardness in an open space, surrounded by other patients who were variously babbling or staring at us blankly, all under the supervision of hospital staff.

Because my days at home with our toddler were long and lonely, I pulled out some of my cookbooks and found a recipe I had never before tackled, nor would I ever tackle it again. It was for baklava, a sticky concoction more at home in the Mediterranean than in my Portland kitchen, I realized, as I battled for hours to create a butter-laden pastry called *mille-feuille* (which translates to "a thousand leaves or layers") that would be patted and folded over nuts and honey and then baked. Any sensible person today would go to the freezer of a grocery store and buy the equivalent puff pastry. Sense was, however, in short supply at this time and I don't know that puff pastry was so readily available in 1967.

After wrapping my creation carefully in aluminum foil, I carried it out to the car. I then dropped our toddler off at a neighbor's house and made the trek up the hill to the psychiatric ward. It's hard to imagine today that the hospital staff would accept a gift of homemade pastry. But they did. And after a sticky intercession, the baklava had disappeared, leaving me to wonder what could be next that night, in a setting that was becoming all too familiar.

Off to one side in the corridor was a ping-pong table. When conversation was at a stalemate, my husband/patient and I picked up the ping-pong paddles and tossed a few balls back and forth. By now, however, in the later stages of my pregnancy, it was becoming difficult to move swiftly and to even get near the ping-pong table.

Perhaps it was the lingering smell of baklava that drew a creature to my kitchen door later that night. I had stopped at the neighbor's house to pick up our child. As we walked up the few steps to the small landing that led through the door into the kitchen, we saw a large, furry creature sitting in a corner. Now, our house stood at the top of a rather steep hill overlooking the Willamette River. This was a very large rodent resembling a giant rat. It was a nutria (in South America known as a *coypu*) that had made its way from the river to our house. (How his ancestors got here originally from South America remains a mystery.) With my child in my arms, I ran across the street to our nearest neighbor, who I thought might have a shotgun. By the time we all returned to the porch, the river rat had disappeared. I never cared for baklava after that night. As a mother of one child and expecting a second, I was not in a position to hate my life. But I could hate river rats. I could dislike going to the psychiatric ward. And I didn't care if ever again I saw or heard of or tasted baklava.

It was several weeks before my husband could leave the hospital. His release came in several phases. His first visit home, just for an afternoon and early evening, was on Thanksgiving. He invited five of his ward mates to join our Thanksgiving table. One woman came into the house, immediately began crying, then hid herself in an upstairs bedroom and didn't come down until it was time for her to return to the hospital. Other visitors congregated with their host in front of the living room fireplace, listening to the Beatles. I was in the kitchen preparing the Thanksgiving feast, wondering what this music was all about. At this time the only music I listened to was classical. Popular culture wasn't part of my world. The mix of a handful of mentally distressed visitors, the to-me alien music in the living room and the simple stress of cooking a turkey overwhelmed me. I went through the motions of cutting and basting and mashing. The turkey and trimmings somehow made it to the table. This day marked the beginning of what eventually would become my own long and painful descent into the abyss of my husband's illness. At about the same time the Beatles entered our house, so did oral sex. When my husband introduced this to our bed one night, I was shocked and perhaps a bit frightened. What were these new ideas coming out of his mania? They were challenging to me. I wondered if I knew him anymore. I wondered how much of what was happening was coming from mental illness — and how much was his true self.

Finally, the day was over. As I cleaned up after the feast amidst occasional outbursts of distress from these visiting patients, I don't recall that I was thankful.

Where Day Begins

When does day begin and sadness fall?
Beyond the line of trees to the clear-cut hill?
At the blanket of pink spread under the magnolia tree?
Through the fog that raised its arms
so the lake could smile and
rocks speak under the spring-rush creek?

Waiting Rooms and Wombs

His release back into the real world took place slowly, over weeks. At first he could go to work and then return to the hospital at night; then he could go to work and come home. The time between Thanksgiving and mid-February, when I went into labor, is a blur. My labor coincided with what I perceived to be his increasing depression, something new to this sick man who was newly home. However, this day he was scheduled to attend a professional conference. He didn't want to go but I suggested he would feel better if he got out of the house and was among professional colleagues. He went, but he had to leave early to take me to the hospital. Infant number two was so eager to be in the world (and out of my stress-fraught womb) that I could barely make it from the hospital parking lot into the maternity ward. There was no time to prep me. The maternity ward was a sanctuary for just a few hours for me and our new baby girl because I was afraid to leave him at home alone with our first-born.

The doctors now had more evidence that led to their eventual conclusion that my husband was suffering from manic-depressive syndrome. The manic side had been front and center since summer. Now with this mood crash came the possibility of suicide. While he did not become an inpatient again at this time, he was fortified by a battery of prescriptions. After being in a drugged state for several months, as he battled depression, he went back in the hospital in a manic state on June 6, 1968, the day Bobby Kennedy was assassinated. At one point during this second, more prolonged hospitalization, his doctor took me aside and advised that unless he started showing some improvement, he would be transferred to the Oregon State Hospital, a psychiatric facility in Salem, a down-market move that would presage a downturn in any hope for recovery. I shuddered. Years ago a professor had assigned my sociology class to visit that facility. My takeaways from that voyage? Don't even think about it. One day, the head of the television station came to the house to inquire about him. I learned that the employment clock was ticking and that he might be terminated.

Meanwhile, the pharmaceutical strategy was to prescribe mood elevators that would lift him out of depression — and when euphoria set in, to administer tranquilizers to bring him down. We were advised that there was a potentially lifesaving treatment that could soon become available. This was lithium, a naturally occurring metal found in grains and vegetables that was still in the experimental phase as a drug to treat bipolar disorder. This treatment would be applied between the highs and lows in hopes of stabilizing upward and downward mood swings. However, lithium was not available to him in the spring of 1968. It would not receive U.S. Food and Drug Administration (FDA) approval until 1970.

Before illness ensnared his mind, his professional reputation had been noteworthy, catching the attention of a public broadcasting company in Manhattan. At that time it was among the country's foremost educational television stations. Shortly after he was released from the hospital the second time around, we were summoned as a couple to attend a function in Portland. The event was held to introduce the powers-that-be from the New York station to the staff at the Portland station. Unbeknownst to us, he was also being scrutinized as a potential addition to the fundraising staff in Manhattan. He received an invitation to join the New York company before the Portland station had decided whether or not to keep him on. Then came the dilemma. Should he share with his potential new employer the state of his mental health? Or should he not? How he handled this was never clear to me. Ethical concerns always disturbed me, including the duplicate government check he received as a uniform allowance when he was in the Army. I insisted he return it.

Within weeks of the job offer, the Manhattan station had whisked this talented man away to Manhattan. He took with him the hope that he could become a guinea pig for lithium treatments. One of the first things he did when arriving in New York was to connect with Bellevue Hospital, which was working with the FDA in assessing the role lithium should play in treating manic-depressive disorder.

Armed with hope that help was just around the corner, I was excited for our new venture and stayed behind with our three-year-old and infant to put the final cosmetic touches on our newly renovated house.

Even as the moving van was dispatched, I was still painting the upstairs bedrooms in this home that had come back to life. The move happened too quickly to put the house on the market, but I did secure tenants. My children and I boarded a plane to begin our life in New York, where husband/father was waiting for us.

A Band

Gypsies came last night, dispossessed my home
and haggled over treasures dearly bought.
They left at sunrise disarray
with more than they had sought.

Crumbling Walls

In the late 1960s we moved our little family from our three-story, four-bedroom house in Portland to a third-floor walk-up on Willow Place in Brooklyn Heights that overlooked the Manhattan skyline. The rent for this apartment was $100 a month. It was called a "walk-up" because there was no elevator. Maneuvering the stairs with grocery cart, stroller, infant and toddler was a several-times-daily challenge.

Ours was the only apartment on the third floor, with one door entering the living room and a fire escape off the room we used as a bedroom. The kitchen looked down into a drab courtyard. A corridor wide enough for a small bed and a crib linked the living room and bedroom. That was where the children slept.

In short order this layout, called a "railroad apartment," was home, with room enough for the piano that had followed me from my childhood home to Portland to Brooklyn Heights. After ten years of piano lessons, I could still play "Für Elise" but not much else.

Conveniently, right next door was a preschool. In 1968 the preschool tuition was $2,000 per year. Here our three-year-old learned to share and socialize for a few hours every day while her baby sister and I ran errands in the neighborhood.

Other reasons for going up and down three flights of stairs several times daily were to walk along the Brooklyn Promenade, swing in a nearby park or amble over to Sahadi's, the purveyor of Middle Eastern foods on Atlantic Avenue. If we walked a few blocks farther, we would come to a grocery that sold live chickens.

Some neighborhoods were dressed with wrought-iron gates. My eldest engaged with such a gate one winter afternoon. The gate closed over her mitten-clad hand. She held the mitten up. When I looked inside the blood-soaked garment, I saw her little thumb dangling. I rushed us down the street, looking for a physician's shingle. One doctor turned us away and sent us to Brooklyn Hospital. This was blocks away. At this time we didn't have a car. On this day, as the thumb was dripping blood, no taxis were available because the drivers were on strike. I stood on a corner desperately waving down cars. A station wagon full of nuns stopped and took us to the hospital. The thumb was stitched back on, leaving no permanent damage.

One night a couple invited us to a party in their apartment, above ours. We went after the children were asleep. I went down every so often to check on them. On one of my descents a heel broke on one of my shoes and I fell almost the whole length of the stairs, cutting my chin on the bottom step. I recall that somehow I caught my mate's attention and that he stood at the top of the stairs staring down at me and not offering assistance. On another evening we were invited across the street to a party. Our hostess had suggested a babysitter, whom we engaged. Upon returning home we found the babysitter sitting in the living room with her boyfriend, and in the morning, in the bathroom wastebasket, we found a sharp tool that resembled a paper cutter. Or was it a knife?

Eventually this life as Sherpa-mother wore thin. The claustrophobia of living with a mentally ill husband became a stress on the load-bearing wall of motherhood. Every night after work he sat at the kitchen table typing out his ideas, which he called "A Theory of Dynamic Unity." Every night I listened and tried to understand his newfound insights into the universe.

My social life in Brooklyn Heights was my husband. The mothers I might say hello to at the park as our children were playing were for the most part engaged in doing the *Atlantic* acrostic or the crossword puzzle in the *New York Times*. They were not interested in chatting. Sometimes on Saturdays I would leave the children with their father and wander about on my own, past the brownstones and boutiques, often mesmerized by arias emanating from open doorways a flight up, thanks to a radio blaring out "Saturday Afternoon at the Opera." This music was my friend, as were books and museums and the haute couture that drew me to elegant windows on Fifth and Madison Avenues.

Playmates were also in short supply for our little girl. One child, a few years older, lived downstairs and sometimes came up to play. When this visitor was expected, my child engaged in a serious search through all of the drawers in the apartment and in every nook and cranny. What was she looking for? Her Barbie doll. Her friend would bring a Barbie doll with her. There was no resident Barbie doll in our house. How to explain to a three-year-old parental preferences for a Madame Alexander doll? Hopefully our denial did not leave a permanent scar.

Why did we trade this apartment for a bungalow on Staten Island? Simply for elbow room and no stairs, and for a backyard that wooed neighborhood children for birthday parties and other celebrations. Hard to believe today, but in 1971 I allowed my first-grader to walk alone the several blocks from our house to Public School 16. One day I was waiting for her after school and met another mother with a young daughter. Soon there was a clutch of young mothers meeting afternoons for coffee, often with mending in our laps, chatting as our children played.

This sociability extended to Christ Church, an Episcopal church in New Brighton. The rector and his wife always opened the rectory's doors for Bloody Marys after church on Sundays, making sure first that the family's pet bunny rabbits wouldn't escape the kitchen. This Sunday ritual was an extension of parties that marked the weekend, beginning often on Friday evening. There were serious times too. The experience of the Right Reverend Paul Moore laying his hands on me during my confirmation at Christ Church went beyond palpable. This flow of energy closed the circle that began with my baptism in Long Beach, California, when I was an infant.

Although roomier than the flat in Brooklyn, our three-bedroom Staten Island cottage covered with wood shingles was not big enough to contain the melee caused by increasingly frequent cycles of one man's highs and lows. The episodes were intensified by alcohol. His manic-depressive disorder gripped us, his wife and children, despite the potentially helpful medicine, lithium, that he received from Bellevue Hospital in Manhattan. He became detached from reality. This put the girls and me at risk one day when he failed to fill the gas tank. The car ran out of gas on the Brooklyn-Queens Expressway. Vapors reached a dew point as I crawled into the back seat with the children, all huddled down on the floor in hopes we could survive if the car was rear-ended. He wandered away to search for gas. Clunkers are so dubbed for a reason. Our car broke down one evening in New Jersey. Rescued by a tow truck, we idled after midnight in a repair shop that housed a snake coiled in an aquarium. Overhead on a lift, another clunker's bolts were shaking from the lovemaking going on in the back seat.

Manic-depressive disorder, a condition that often rears its ugly head in young adulthood (my mate was twenty-nine), had, it seems, been predicted seven years earlier by the physician who examined both of us before our wedding. I did not know about this family doctor's prognosis until years later — too late, obviously, to change my mind about marrying him or bearing his children. Had I known the toll this illness would take on me and our children, would I have walked down that aisle? I remember that a little twinge had made me halt on my father's arm. *Do I really want to commit my life to this man?* I'd wondered. But guests were sitting out there in front of us, expecting that the show would go on.

In this era there were no effective pharmaceutical treatments for manic-depressive disorder. As a "test" patient at Belleview Hospital, even after he'd ingested the new panacea, lithium, his manic episodes began leading him down alleys far removed from his own strict Missouri Synod Lutheran upbringing. Although I was expanding my own cultural horizons, I was far from worldly. I had no experience with which to judge his new behaviors, which included extramarital affairs and experiments with *ménages à trois* (I wasn't around for those), along with what he described as the possibility of a homosexual engagement with his barber. This was Manhattan in the early 1970s.

He was oblivious to his daughters and to me as he scribbled manically at night and performed for National Educational Television by day, sourcing support for *Sesame Street* and hitting up companies like Mobil to sponsor *Masterpiece Theatre*. Fundraising at that level was like being inside a pressure cooker. When after-hours drinking was stirred in, the lid blew. The potent mix of mental illness and alcohol, and the possibility that he had taken himself off of lithium because he missed the highs, caught up with him. I soon learned that for several weeks he had only been pretending to go into the office. He had been fired and we needed to get out of Dodge.

Throughout, I tried to be a loyal mate, typing up his ideas. He believed his manuscript would be the panacea for all the problems of the world. Mr. Dick came out of the fog. Mr. Dick's lifework as a character from the pages of *David Copperfield* was to write the history of King Charles' beard. The light bulb came on. I shut my eyes and kept on typing.

An Ancient Lesson

Penelope pursued patiently
the personal penance projected
to posit in perspective
her perpetual plight of loneliness
prolonged due to peregrinations
of quaint Ulysses who quarreled
with the quadrants of the world,
quelling disasters to qualify himself
as a quick quencher of adversity.
The moral: Mind your p's and q's.

Gasping for Air

Was this "take a deep breath" time or more like "gasping for air" time? I don't recall.

When my husband finally got around to telling me he had been fired, I updated my resume, which at that point included only one year of teaching. After submitting my information to a temporary employment agency, I arrived on the top floor of the skyscraper dubbed the Socony-Mobil Building located on 42nd Street near Grand Central Station in Manhattan. Across the hush of carpeted floors I was directed to serve coffee to a man on whose door I always knocked but who was oblivious as my hand shook under the cup and saucer of fine china that I held out to him. Here I was to type correspondence on thick, creamy letterhead, embossed, of course. This paper I deemed so expensive that when I made a typing error I would pull the paper from the Selectric typewriter, crumple the paper up and stuff it into my purse, lest someone see the expensive vellum paper in the wastebasket.

The view from this aerie was stunning, overlooking Manhattan and the harbor. But my gaze was only on maintaining this temporary secretarial position so that money could continue to flow into the household. One afternoon while I was boarding the southbound train for Lower Manhattan out of Grand Central Station, the crush of the city sent me into an elevated state of panic. I forgot which stop on the subway line was mine. My distress became evident to a man standing next to me on the train. At the next stop he guided me off the train and into the stagnant air of the underground maze. Here he was able to elicit a response from me and directed me to the train I needed. Then he disappeared.

Meanwhile, the world I had been propping up on Staten Island was not functioning. Two little girls, ages seven and five, needed care. Their father neglected any semblance of maintaining order around the house as he worked on his "A Theory of Dynamic Unity" manuscript. Last night's dishes, along with the day's breakfast and lunch dishes, were still in the sink when I came home. The stack of untidiness grew ever higher as his manuscript grew thicker. My requests that he begin dinner preparations went unheeded. After dinner, when the girls were in bed, he would review with me the progress he had made that day on his manuscript.

Even though he no longer had an office to report to, he kept up a few contacts from his now-past professional life. His friend Steve also experienced the extreme highs and lows that come with manic-depressive disorder. In one of his manic episodes, Steve purchased one hundred white roses and flew to Israel to present them to Golda Meir, who at this time was the prime minister of Israel. Along with the roses, this scheme wilted. Steve's wife appeared to manage her husband's episodes with efficacy, a talent I did not share. On the surface she seemed to be a partner to her husband, despite his idiosyncrasies. Both of them were highly attuned to their only son, an aspiring actor. Perhaps their adoration for their son was the glue that kept her stuck to her husband. Meanwhile, our two little ones continued to have play dates with their friends. We still went to Christ Church on Sundays, where the girls attended Sunday school. Whatever had seemed normal in their lives continued, but I now left the house every day with the hope that they would be OK when I returned.

Another couple we entertained came with the trappings of eccentricity and enough wealth to furnish their Long Island home in a style reminiscent of *Architectural Digest*. They visited us one day at our Staten Island bungalow. My menu was cheese soufflé followed by custard. Harry told us about his heart issues. His wife called the next day to say that Harry had died of a heart attack that night. For years I felt guilty about what I thought might have been the undesired results of having served this cholesterol-laden meal. Only a later saga about attempts to fulfill Harry's wishes to have his ashes scattered on the Isle of Skye assuaged my guilt. Far worse things were in store for Harry. His ashes were lost en route to the destination and Scotland Yard was called in for the search. I didn't make a cheese soufflé for some time after that, as the image of Harry bobbing about in a box at sea drifted across my mind.

Working as a temp secretary for an employment agency was not lucrative. The one-time breadwinner's severance pay was soon used up. We could not continue to pay the mortgage on our Staten Island bungalow. A few years earlier we had enjoyed a ski vacation in Vermont. We thought that Vermont would be a lovely place to live and certainly it would be cheaper than continuing to live in New York on very little money.

Our Staten Island bungalow was soon in the hands of a real estate company and we were in the hands of a real estate agent in Vermont. By now each of us was incapable of exercising logic. As the Vermont real estate agent unfurled possibilities before us, I was still rational enough to know that owning a ski lodge, charming as it sounded, would be at best an "iffy" enterprise. But a country store? That was something else entirely. People needed to eat twelve months of the year.

The day came to pack up a U-Haul for a venture north to what would be our new home, the East Poultney General Store on the edge of a Vermont village green where a mandolin factory had long since shut its doors. One famous person who lived here was Horace Greeley. As an apprentice he learned the printing trade while living in East Poultney, before becoming editor of the *New York Herald Tribune* and in 1872 a Presidential candidate. He also advised, "Go West, young man, go West." As the West was where we had come from, perhaps we should have heeded his advice.

Today's fly-now, pay-later mentality serves to shrink time and distance and doubtless does keep families and friends better connected. In the 1970s hopping on an airplane was still a luxury. And where would we have gone, anyway? His family was in distress, his mother in the grip of Lou Gehrig's disease. His father was in the grip of bureaucracy, as he had been ordered from his home by eminent domain exercised by Oregon State University's bid to extend its campus in Corvallis, Oregon. My mother would soon suffer a serious stroke. Shortly after we moved to East Poultney she died, having wished me "good luck" on what was to be her last telephone call to me. My father made do alone on the farm until my brother and his wife invited him to join their household in Medford, Oregon.

The four of us piled into the U-Haul and headed north, skyscrapers disappearing behind us as the Berkshires gave way to the Taconics that handed themselves over to the Green Mountains. In the U-Haul, I turned over and over and over again in my mind possibilities for earning a living should the country store enterprise, into which we had plunged all we possessed, betray us. Sewing, I decided, would be a skill I could always depend on. While growing up on a farm I had honed my domestic skills through 4-H. After ten years in this organization, my skills as a seamstress were those of a couturier. The only thing I didn't know how to do was to create a garment from cloth draped over a mannequin. Years later, on a business trip to Ottawa, I wandered into an atelier where the proprietor was doing just that. I asked if he ever tutored in this skill. The answer was "yes," but I never got back to Ottawa.

The ride north to Vermont was long and tiring. My mind was racing. I never once considered what I would sew, or for whom I would sew, only that I could sew. As it turned out I never had to poke a needle into the household economy, probably because I never knew where we stood financially. There were no spreadsheets at the country store. Solvency, if not success, was indicated by whether or not there was cash in the cash drawer in the old-fashioned, manually operated cash register. This was the star of the store and certainly the *pièce de résistance* for our out-of-town guests. By focusing on the cash register it was easy to overlook the rough-hewn wooden floors that would never take kindly to a mop and barely endured a broom sweep. Several aisles of metal shelving were magnets for the dust that emanated from the old floors. One of my duties was to dust the shelves and the tins of food stacked on the shelves. Things would go smoothly for me until I hit the row laden with tuna fish cans. These little devils didn't like to be stacked. One afternoon, tired of picking up cans that had toppled onto the floor, I took my hand and brushed it down the shelf. The sound of can after can after can toppling to the floor and the sight of them then rolling into oblivion was some kind of catharsis for me. I only did this once. I picked them all back up and settled them in stacks and hated tuna fish thereafter.

Beyond the center aisles were shelves on the left that displayed cleaning and drinking products. To the right was the deli counter. Iterations of meat with strange-sounding names were lined up in lumps inside the counter, along with a few assorted cheeses. The store did not carry fresh meats, only iterations thereof that were so laden with salts and preservatives that I felt guilty selling them.

Friends from Manhattan were happy to come visit us in what to them — and always to us — was the exotic setting of East Poultney, Vermont. One guest delighted in running the cash register that sat on top of the glass-topped counter, which displayed candy and an assortment of colorful pocket knives. We had purchased the store's inventory when we bought the business and had no way of knowing how important knives were — or were not. Some things we didn't reorder, but the candy purveyor was at our door every week.

The children loved sneaking candy from the candy counter. Our youngest was prone to a poor appetite and a sickly-sweet breath that can only be blamed on the candy counter. Overtime the families we were closest to on Staten Island found their way to our door. Each visit recreated momentarily the joy we first experienced in moving to the Green Mountains. Our flamboyant apartment over the store sported an orange paisley wallpaper in the dining room and a blue paint that nods to Yankee in the living room. Flowers, dried come winter, and candlelight drew new and far-flung friends for an occasional salon. My husband rose to the occasion for these events and was a charming host, as long as he wasn't steering the conversation to King Charles' beard.

Meanwhile I indulged in a kind of domestic therapy by baking daily eighteen loaves of bread (three batches at a time) in the oven of our upstairs apartment. As a girl on my family's farm I had become proficient in the art of baking. The impetus for this proficiency was first to fulfill the expectations that 4-H laid forth. My participation over ten years in this organization led to my bread being entered at the Lane County Fair. I didn't score high enough in bread baking to get to the next rung on the ladder, the Oregon State Fair. Another impetus for becoming proficient in baking had a more sinister twist. Years later I realized that my father had been the focus of my culinary efforts. Now, my mother was an excellent cook. But she didn't deliver freshly baked cookies and lemonade to him in the field, as I did. A little Electra complex going on here, probably.

Then, as now, bread was a marketing ploy. At the store I was delivering fragrant loaves hot out of the oven to the countertop downstairs as farmers and laborers came in for last-minute, end-of-day shopping. This bread was not a moneymaker, however, because the flour we purchased wholesale for our store, in the small quantities dictated by demand, was still more expensive than what I could buy at the local IGA, a mile down the road toward Poultney.

Come Friday afternoons, my husband emptied this cash register before disappearing for the weekend to places like Canada, questing after such gurus as Krishnamurti. The value of our investment in the store was dwindling. The savings account and the insurance policies that we had plundered to purchase the 1830 structure that was also our home were long gone. We were dependent on the store for our livelihood — and for our home. Only the fact that we could purchase for the children crates of strawberries and whatever other fresh fruit might be available consoled me at this time. Even the patchwork placemats I stitched up to sell in the store — and my handcrafted cotton dolls with yarn hair, which looked like models for children's story books as they sat there in the store window — provided only momentary diversion. The fact that these created-by-hand items didn't sell was annoying. But I've since noticed that similar supplication to the merchandising clichés of country stores and rural, old-fashioned living don't sell today in Vermont. Although hope and fudge still do.

What did sell? Pickled eggs that looked like eyeballs floating in an unknown liquid in gallon jugs; deli meats, the likes of which I had never sampled before, then or since; lots of Old Duke and Red Rose wines (this was long before the days that good wines were stocked on the shelves of Vermont country stores); Budweiser and Schlitz; potato chips; white bread; cigarettes; chewing tobacco that contributed to the illusion that a lot of men in East Poultney had constant toothaches; and wedges of Crowley cheese. I took great pride in being able to slice this cheese into exact pounds.

Every few months I drove the winding forty-four miles from East Poultney to Healdville, Vermont, home since 1881 of the Crowley Cheese Company. This drive wound me away from my village green and provided an escape from the store's constant demands. The route also led to the grounds of a religious order where Benedictine monks reside. Here I was unceremoniously turned away late one afternoon as winter was closing in. I knocked on the priory door, ready to ask for something I didn't even know I needed: practical and spiritual guidance on how to extricate me and the children from an increasingly challenging situation. Women turning up at the priory's doorstep to ask for help was perhaps an anomaly. Whoever answered the door closed it quickly in my face, before I'd even stated my mission, leaving me to wind my way back to East Poultney, to two little girls and to one very sick man.

What brought some people into the store at this time was the newly instituted, compulsory bottle return law. This law furthered Vermont's progress as a state free of eyesores that continued to infect other parts of the country. On the local level this law translated to handing over refunds of nickels and dimes to those who brought in bottle after sticky bottle and can after stale-smelling can. The cans and bottles were then sorted by brand into cases the delivery men would retrieve. This sorting ritual took place in the dirt basement under the store. This chore fell to me when there was no husband around and as the children slept upstairs.

One evening the world caved in around me. I was crouched in the basement on my haunches, hot and getting dirtier by the minute. The jumble of bottle and cans that had been opened and returned seemed endless. The process of sorting them into cardboard boxes by brand seemed a waste of time. My pent-up fury at finding myself squatting over foul-smelling residuals of other people's lives exploded. I sent one bottle after another crashing against the basement supports as I screamed to any rodents that happened to make their home here: "This is not why I have a degree from Stanford! This is not why I have a degree from Stanford." The rage might have been invoked by my discovery of a dead rodent in one of the bottles. It didn't take much.

When the father and husband returned after his days and nights away, he resumed his duties as manager of the store and I went back to baking cookies, pies and bread. The little girls were protected from the widening schism between their parents. They loved the nightly ritual of listening to bedtime stories that he spun for them. The tension of intellectual, emotional and by-now physical distance took its toll on both of us, and in one unfortunate episode, his anger erupted as a clenched fist slammed against my left ear. My reaction? Something like, "Oh, that just happened. Did he really just do that?" I was horrified. Where do I find the box that fits this? I was numb. My ear was ringing. I don't recall that I even reacted, for fear of exacerbating his out-of-control anger. This blow was a game changer. I had gone from the person trying to manage our family and his illness to the object of his violence.

The store wasn't at fault. Mental illness was. We were. We had invested everything we owned in an effort to rescue a sinking ship — not only the store but in this case a marriage and family. This strategy probably never solves any problems. Like the boogie man in a bad dream, the problem, the mental illness, never went away. The absences of father, husband and storekeeper became more frequent and longer, and the money became tighter, until finally love's labor lost. He went away.

The Departure

Absence makes the heart grow fonder.
Stay away a little longer.

Move Over, Mrs. Dalloway

This troubled man began writing "A Theory of Dynamic Unity" in 1967 while in the psychiatric ward in Portland, Oregon. Five years later, having blown through Manhattan and Staten Island, he was in a village in Vermont, still pondering how he would save the world through his writing.

Meanwhile I was growing increasingly detached from any interest in his ideas. Early on I would focus on his far-ranging monologues and later type up his hand-written notes. As one who suffered from "the good wife" syndrome, I tried to understand his ideas and was willing to follow him — up to a point. Today I don't have a clue what that point was. Did my detachment begin when I shared with him my enthusiasm one day for the beauty of a particularly blue sky and his response was to parse the concept of blue? Suddenly life, already complicated, became more so and I began to keep my distance from his mental gyrations. This led naturally to fewer conversations about anything, because my stomach would knot when a perfectly ordinary observation I might make could be lassoed and spun into his own orbits. To preserve my own sanity I had to stay away from those orbits.

British author Virginia Woolfe figures prominently in the pantheon of English literature. Her novel *Mrs. Dalloway* offers observations of two characters: Rezia, a wife, and her husband, Septimus, who suffers a mental illness. I needed a way to distance myself from my own realities. Inspired by Woolfe and while reflecting on the fragility and disintegration of relationships, including my marriage, I wrote "Move Over, Mrs. Dalloway." At this time we still lived as a family unit in the light-filled apartment over the country store in East Poultney. I remember the little unused bedroom with bunkbeds and the heavy wooden desk with a Royal typewriter (the truly old-fashioned, manual version, with an inked ribbon) on which I worked. I remember rustling through my husband's scribblings, many of which I had typed, to gather my material. What follow are the husband's words, directly from his writings. The dialogue of the wife, Sara, is added as counterpoint, which hopefully communicates to families experiencing the tragedy of mental illness that those of us left behind are not alone. Left unacknowledged is the villain of this drama, mental illness. Villains can force people into becoming what they would never want to be. This villain challenged two people in a still-young and hopeful marriage, making a laughingstock of "in sickness and in health." This villain evoked fear and potential danger and eventually disarmed any possibility that the man the woman married, who disappeared into the arms of the villain, would ever reappear as his old self. The only bit characters to appear on our stage were turmoil and tragedy.

Sara: You are weary. Close your eyes and rest. Shall I tell your story for you? Give me your diary. In boxes in the closet and in piles around the room. Manuscripts on yellow sheets. For seven years you've tried so long to tell your tale. Are your diaries in order? Is there sequence to your writing, clipping, and marking and the newspapers with scribbled notes? What do they mean?

Husband: My mind rushes after three Scotches on the rocks that will have me racing with sleep or stupor in an hour from now. But finally I have begun. I have written the first words, and I'll be damned if I'll change them. They say exactly what this book is all about — THE YELLOW DOUGHNUT. Since I came here I have broken all the Bible's Ten Commandments either actually or in my mind. Where have you arrived when you stop wondering how your memorized bits of pieces of life began and when you only wonder that they have not ended? What kind of creature are you when you no longer indulge by bracketing yourself between two logical fallacies, the concepts of beginnings and endings against by which you have been taught since birth to measure your version of truth?

Sara: So many beginnings. But you say that is a fallacy, that what you are writing never really begins, or, according to truth, never can end. So I read excerpts, bits and pieces of you straining for a whole. What does "yellow doughnut" mean?

Husband: Going through the motions. At the age of twenty-nine a profound change in consciousness occurred, which made me see myself as a symbolic presence of life, a symbol of various kinds of action played out among the living. As a result of thinking in these terms, I discovered what I describe as the other end of the symbolic continuum: the concept of soul.

Sara: And where did that lead?

Husband: JESUS CHRIST FOUND IN PSYCHIATRIC WARD. My wife could not believe that she had married the Son of God, had borne him a daughter and was five months pregnant with his second child.

Sara: I was happy carrying your children. I remember the joy of love on the pine needles in the woods, and I laughed because I knew it could happen. The baby was perfect and fat. The second time was tiring. I was cross after a year of teaching and studying and tending the baby. You were working hard on the house. A carpenter at heart and a painstaking craftsman, you left your office night after night to come home to bring love to us in an old house. You worried, though, about your mother, ill of an unknown disease. Have I ever told you that in the end she reminded me of Lazarus? I was impatient with sickness and death, as the young must be. She interfered with us by troubling you, you who could not help but who could only mourn her pain. I should have comforted you, held you in your sorrow, but I was full of your baby, impatient to be on with life and so I turned my back in fear.

Husband: By pleasant coincidence and not by design, the inner circle turns out to be a peace symbol when man is superimposed upon the circle. When man finds his balance point in the circle, he understands life and can exist in peace.

Sara: Your head whirled with ideas, eager to pursue the studies of your past and then apply them to facts about our world. A magazine perhaps? We both would share inception and production of ideas. Distribution, layout, articles, travel, meetings, schedules, budgets, critics, books, films. You are not sleeping. Why can't you get to sleep? Fix yourself some warm milk. What are you doing with all of those books? The great ideas of man? You did not sleep again last night. What are you staring at from the window? The stars are out. Shall we go downstairs and drink warm milk? Let's sit here. I will bring you all of our shoes and we can polish shoes. That will take your mind off not being able to sleep. It's 3:00 a.m. Polish, polish.

Husband: We left our old grey Peugeot in a downhill parking lot below the hospital. It was Saturday, the Jewish Sabbath, and somehow we made it from our house to the psychiatric ward without accomplishing an important mission. I was to make a surprise visit to a little synagogue, round and shiny-domed like the head of a circumcised penis. There I would announce that I had risen if not for the second time then at least for the first. Dressed in my dark blue suit purchased from a Jewish friend, I would show them the scars on my hands. I knew that once they saw the scars and saw how forgiving I was, I would be put on third base and heading for home plate as the New Messiah!

For the past week my wife has not understood me. She was anxious. How anxious, I was unable to see because of my own personal elation.

"Look at my hands," I said to her as we approached the hospital. "See these scars."

I had impetigo as a child. Remember that. She did not reply but looked at me, hurt, as if someone had slipped a knife through her stomach. I was shaken by her face only to consider that while the nail in my left hand had been a dead bull's-eye, the Roman soldier crippling my right hand had actually botched the job. As the scar indicated, the nail was in the lower V between my thumb and index finger. There must have been enough flesh around the nail to hold my limp body without the right hand tearing away. It was a lousy job, and I almost chuckled thinking about that poor sonofabitch private who had to pound in the nail. I was once an Army officer and I know the whole routine. From this very creative relationship between the officer and the man in the ranks, little work of high quality results.

We were still walking. I was floating. Things were unfolding I had never imagined I could conceive of, let alone understand. In the space of a few days I had discovered a rationale for loving everyone in the world. When I discovered I was Christ, of course, that capped it off nicely. But how in God's name could Christ sleep? I lay in bed with toothpick eyes staring into blackness where paths of light became geometric forms and simple lines and curves. No sleep in four days made me fuzzy. I was falling behind schedule. But, fuzzy mind, the words had not yet come, and Christ chose to enter a psychiatric ward to preserve his sanity. Peace be still.

Sara: You needed sleep. The doctors promised to put you to sleep at the hospital so you could rest for your work. That is how we got you to go — for sleep.

Husband: What a gas! This whole thing is reading out like it's programmed for a computer. I've been told to report to Dr. Bishop at the psychiatric ward. Christ appears before Bishop. With a small, lightly packed suitcase, I entered Ward 6 at the hospital. I have little or no anxiety about entering as a patient.

Sara: You entered to rest. And to write. You planned to work on your book there. And you wrote and slept, drugged. Friends visited you. Some thought you were spoofing. I searched madly for labels and books on the mind. Your doctors asked me if you had been on LSD. Acutely psychotic, paranoid, schizophrenic. You were all in one, according to the diagnosis. The doctors who gave you drugs locked you in a cell with just a hole for observation and a vista of the valley, through barred windows. You said they had to wrestle you to give a shot. After you slept, you wanted to come home. But you stayed for weeks. We played ping-pong in the halls, remember? I came up every night, shifting my growing bulk around that wooden ping-pong table, trying to laugh in the open ward. I brought you cookies and communiques from all your friends who cared (and who were afraid their minds, too, might blow).

Husband: I realized that my thinking of late had been almost totally concerned with life and behavior and communication systems. Much of this I can relate to the constant speed of light in that light provides for man today the most reliable aspect from which he can see his individual and collective truths. I am bored with mulling over great ideas. I'm fighting this boredom by stating contrasts rather than making things factual. No one understands the explosiveness of this peaceful idea in my mind. I do but cannot talk about it because my plodding mind has not yet sniffed out all the relationships embodied in the idea. I can feel the electricity almost as though my brain circuits are closed and fully conductive. There seems to be some difficulty in determining which language the program is written in.

Sara: You are depressed. Don't just lie there. Why don't you get up? Spade the garden. We want to plant grass in the spring.

Husband: Writing is a lonely and boring task. Although it may not be replaced for a long time, I feel that it is a dying form of communication. Perhaps it will be revived in some form of computerized shorthand that will allow man to reason with symbols, test his logic, alter or state fact, then relay what he knows in equally communicable form to a broader audience.

Sara: Do you think the baby will come soon? Please don't lie there. I want the baby to come. Maybe you will feel better with new life around. The baby is coming. Please, get up.

Husband: The three-sided approach to past, present and future shows no relationship between the three realms of man's conception save arbitrary connections and the points of the triangle. In the triangle we place a circle. Next comes man. His presence throws the whole symbolic scene delightfully off balance. In contact with the future, past and present are his hands, and his feet are planted where that electric spark of life that is in him once mixed past with present.

Sara: You left triangles all over the house. Etched in plasterboard and poked with nails into casings. Drawn on telephone books. Even peas were lined up in triangles on your plate.

Husband: Day is done. Gone the sun. Goeth day. Cometh night. And a star leadeth all, speedeth all to their rest.

Sara: Will you sleep now? I'm glad the baby is another girl. I wonder what would have happened had she been a boy?

Husband: The roots of the tree of life are embedded in instinctive fear. Trying to invade the territory of a man's mind, telling him how to think. The more blatant the intrusion becomes, the more aggressive will be the counter-blow in defense of an individual's mental freedom.

Sara: But I don't tell you how to think. I do resent your interpreting everything I say in the light of present, past and future and man churning in your triangles. I have babies to feed.

Husband: Understanding is a relative thing. Minds are like snowflakes. Each mind has its own picture of the world, one that has never been painted before nor will be again.

Sara: Will you stop? I am tired.

Husband: Nothing ever lived without a sense of space, or time, and nothing imagined ever lived without. What I wish to get at is our insistence on taking polar positions in time and space while completely ignoring the relative motions of things. We must relate the tight and loose through new awareness of the meaning of our sensory perceptions. I have emigrated, not by skill, but by a blend of chance and necessity to a new land of elation and joy tempered with memory of past experience and with future possibilities that I imagine.

Sara: I understand. Are you resting? It has been such a long time since you slept. What do you mean by the yellow doughnut?

FINI

Icarus

Icarus in flight toward the sun
treads upon the primal
source, allows hands to rest,
lovely child, on my breast.
Still strength flows through tired men,
bosoms nourish, comfort.
Mother's milk destroys Icarus,
angry, snapping like bees caught
feasting on a blooming hedge.
Tears on my cheek, nectar of his dreams,
moustache tickles nipples as we sleep.

When Shoes Fit

The worlds of selling merchandise and foodstuffs were new to me except for a brief stint serving customers when I found myself in Long Branch, New Jersey, with nothing to do but cook while my husband continued his military training at Fort Monmouth, New Jersey.

One afternoon, bored, I put on a summer suit and pumps and wandered past storefronts. The first business to catch my eye was the office of a nearly defunct weekly newspaper published by a Mr. Bobbitt. Yes, he would hire me. For what I don't remember, but I must have done some small piece of reporting for which he exchanged one silver dollar. Perhaps he thought I was a grandchild. Remember, this was 1960 and Mr. Bobbitt was very old.

When Mr. Bobbitt could no longer figure out how to use my talents, a "Help Wanted" sign caught my eye. I was hired on the spot to sell shoes in a shoe store for the weeks until we sailed to Italy. My parents never knew that their carefully cultivated daughter was on her knees helping people try on shoes. Even though it had been okay for these parents to send me out to the milking parlor once monthly to scrub manure-stained walls and to see me on my knees scrubbing the farmhouse kitchen and dining room floors, for them to visualize their daughter on her knees before the world just wasn't going to happen. In fact, by remaining silent about my activities, I was protecting my father from his prejudices.

As a teen I had devoured magazine profiles of young women, seemingly always blonde, working their way up to fame and glory in retail, folding and refolding lovely sweaters and caressing garments clinging to hangars on the periphery. Kneeling before people didn't faze me. Stacking the shoe boxes and sourcing sizes and colors did. Retail held no allure for me. Now I understood my preference for doing farm chores and picking beans in a neighbor's bean yard. (See my first memoir, *The Dusky Afternoon: An Oregon Childhood*.)

Now once again engaged in retail, this time in a Vermont village and married — sort of — I felt compelled to expand the family's solvency beyond what the cash register drawer could deliver. I needed a credit card, which could only be issued by a bank. And the bank would only issue a card if I had a bank officer vouch for me. At the time, one of the officers of a bank in nearby Rutland was a successful real estate mogul, a woman, who met me at the bank and put me to shame. My garb had turned to pre–Ralph Lauren hippie and she was dressed in a wool suit befitting Fifth Avenue. But she gave her approval to the bank to grant me a card.

Deserted in the East Poultney General Store and with dependent children, I was left hanging in the wind. How long could this last? The floating eyeballs never left the counter. The rats were at home in bottles waiting to be sorted in the dank earth basement. I couldn't stomach the stench of the deli meats. And my at-home therapy, bread baking, went by the wayside because I couldn't be in the kitchen upstairs and at the cash register downstairs at the same time. My desperation led to a flurry of phone calls from the wall phone in the store while I was on cashier duty one morning. In search of a safety net of any kind, I called the local recruiting offices of whichever branches of the military answered their phones in Rutland, Vermont. My question was a simple one. If I were to enlist, could I be guaranteed entry as an officer, not as an enlisted person? Haunting me were memories of two years on the Mediterranean and another year near Heidelberg. The military offered security. My children would be safe. The recruiters could offer no guarantees. Taking the chance of ranking lower than my own self-esteem wasn't in the cards. The quest for order and security ended, but the shadows still inhabit family lore: "Remember when Mommy tried to join the Army?" This outreach made my youngest daughter cry.

The girls and I soldiered on at the store, serving customers. When the cash register was quiet, we created Christmas ornaments of felt and glue and sequins. The sparkles stuck. This lifestyle didn't.

For all intents and purposes, the man of the house had permanently disappeared, leaving chance to walk through the door of the store one day with an offer for me to become editor of a weekly newspaper that heralded the touristic virtues of the greater Rutland, Vermont, region. I returned for a fourth time to a newspaper engagement. The first had been my summer job just out of high school as a reporter on the

Springfield Reporter in Springfield, Oregon. The second was serving on the newspaper staff of a daily newspaper while in college. The third was the silver-dollar stint with Mr. Bobbitt. Now the fourth would introduce me to life on yet another version of the flying carpet. This iteration was homespun, revealing Vermont and people and history and happenings about which I came to write and photograph weekly. I solicited writers to submit their musings to me. They were happy to do this for free. A professor at a local college wrote a weekly column on the geology of the region. A neighbor provided her favorite recipes. I canvassed main and back roads for interesting stories and camera-perfect pictures. People loved *The Reporter*. I paid to play by selling advertisements to support my stipend. Did the publisher break even? I didn't have a clue, until the paper folded.

By then my byline was recognizable within a small radius of East Poultney. A colleague introduced me to the marketing guru of a major ski resort in Vermont. He hired me to do public relations for this rapidly expanding company. I hired a manager to run the store, checking in occasionally to see that the business was solvent. When I was called to Oregon for my mother's funeral, I directed the store manager to hold a sale that would effectively shut down the store. He did, and the customers who used to come in for white bread and potato chips and to collect dimes and nickels for soda and beer bottles and cans moved on down the road to the IGA after scarfing up tins of canned salmon and jars of capers at my now dirt-cheap prices. Not until years later, after I sold the building, did the store re-open.

Aphrodisias

We left the sea behind
lovely as the leaves littering paths
from temple to agora,
remarking along the way
the Asian poplar,
yellow against the squall
sending us to shelter
under a pomegranate tree.

People Parade

The country store did offer me unexpected dividends. I had for a few years a front-row seat to the comedy — and tragedy — of village life in East Poultney. As people's stories rolled by me every day, I came to understand the courage that must be mustered to be always cheerful, which the delivery men were as they wrestled their trolleys through my doorway to stock the shelves. Then there were the customers. One cranky old man came in every afternoon after his day on the job. He still had to work at age seventy-five because he was the breadwinner for his wife and her ninety-something-year-old parents, who lived with them. One farmer, who brought back from Vietnam a permanent limp, was the father of a brood of towheads. He transacted with food stamps and shared with me his hopes of salvaging the family dairy farm, hidden somewhere over there near the granite quarries.

Then there was the hermit. I would watch him from the store's rear window, looking out over the cornfield, and I can still see him walking down the road. He comes into view when he's a half mile or so away, where the road takes a sharp bend up there by the gorge. In the summer the lush, almost tropical foliage of trees and brush obscures him until he's near the cemetery. Come winter, such thin and lonely forms as his are sharp against the snow.

He doesn't take long to pass the cemetery where many people of the village, mostly Protestant, claim ancestors that were laid to rest. Beyond the knoll and across the dead-end road, there's another plot, with new graves, all fenced around and Jewish. As folks tell it, it's unusual in a small New England town to find such a Jewish cemetery. Initially Jews came here, they say, as tinkers, selling what couldn't be crafted, forged or spun locally. And down at the bottom of the main cemetery, all by himself, rests a slave who had served his master in the Civil War. The master is buried farther up.

Israel Brown, walking down the road, doesn't pause to mark the graves. Now on his left is the willow in the cornfield, a bird of foreign plumage that stands solitary like a bark riding the waves of summer corn; but this bird is melancholy as the shorn field settles down for a long wait before redwing blackbirds and crows flock back in the spring.

Now I can see the old canvas bag Israel carries, a two-handled affair. In another few minutes he will come into the store. He's just passing a garden owned by Lewis, a bachelor who always gifted us a box of chocolates at Christmas. The garden that Lewis tends yields tender peas and plump strawberries, and later beans and other yield of summer, including blackberries. Not far from this small farm is the post office, attached to the house of the postmistress, who sells raspberries and whose proclivity for tippling is hardly a secret since the smell of whiskey often wafts through the transaction window over to the customer.

Israel is out of sight momentarily behind the grand yellow house, a well-preserved and historic tavern next door to the store. There, it's rumored, Ethan Allen and the Green Mountain Boys gathered over ale in the stone cellar to plot strategies against, among others, the British. The local boys were defending their beginning-to-be-established farms and communities, both from the British during the Revolutionary War and from others, south in New York territory, who laid a claim to this land north of the New Hampshire grants. In fact, a several-times-over great-grandfather, John R. Cobb, of Clarendon and Charlotte, Vermont, probably knew this house. And there's no question that Ethan's cousin, Colonel Ebenezer Allen, was a frequent visitor while he was helping develop the town that became Poultney, Vermont. I didn't know until decades later, after hours on Ancestry.com, that John R. Cobb is my third great-grandfather and that Ebenezer Allen is my fifth great-granduncle.

Looking back to the hermit: Israel comes to the crossroads on the green, passes the Johnson's Eagle Tavern and finally comes into the store. He never stays long, just long enough to buy what he needs to keep him for a month or so. The food he purchases is substantial, the staples hunters or fishermen might toss in with their beer: tins of Dinty Moore beef stew and corned beef, coffee, and tins of vegetables and fruits. If he hunts or fishes or traps, I don't know. I only see him and know of him when he comes to the store to make his infrequent transactions or as he walks up and down the short stretch of road around the village green.

He always pays in cash. No food stamps or credit slips or checks. As he carefully counts out bills, there's still money left in his coin purse when the purchase is made. What he relinquishes for food is not, then, his last nickel. His clothing tells a different story. He wears an old, dark tweed jacket, loose and ill-fitting and yet worn with the kind of dignity that says he might have owned the jacket when it was, at one time, new. The pants are also dark and smudgy, and he wears a cap, resembling the button-down style worn with a duster in an open touring car.

His hair is dark, his skin tawny, his fingernails dirty and his eyes veiled. The transaction is over quickly and silently, after he walks first among the island of food, picking up a tin here and a tin there and using his canvas bag as a shopping cart. When he comes to the counter the bag must be unloaded. The first time I repacked the cans into a paper bag, carefully putting items in one at a time so he could balance the load (because I knew he had to walk several miles back to his home). He let me pack all the items before saying he prefers to have everything in the canvas bag. I emptied out the paper and started again.

It's always a trick to set the groceries around the old newspapers and whatever else he has packed in there. The contents of the bag, like a medicine chest, arouse my curiosity. Although sturdy enough, it is dirty and smells smoky. Then, as the canvas bag bulges (and it weighs enough by now, too), he carries it out the door. There's little or no exchange between us. Perhaps a routine "How are you?" from me. But he never more than looks at me from the corner of his eye, wary, not quite saying "Buzz off, lady!" but as close as a person can come when he wants to be left alone and doesn't intend to meet routine comment with routine comment.

I do not think he is rude; in fact, his seeming lack of interest in social amenities and his attention to the transactions (executed in remarkable silence on his part) only makes my remarks seem like intruders on his stark world, a silent one devoid of pleasantries.

When he leaves the store he walks on down the road, sometimes getting a ride from a passing driver who recognizes him as a neighbor, although he never solicits help. He's on his way to the railroad tracks farther down in Poultney, where people say he picks up pieces of coal that have spilled from the train cars, packing the coal into his pockets and around the groceries in the canvas bag. This is what he used to do when the coal cars still came through town.

Sometimes he does not stop here on his path to the coal, but he walks all the way down the street, a mile or so, to a larger market. I have a strange feeling that when he passes by here he does not trust me to keep my mouth shut should he come inside — that I will challenge his silence, like an unwelcome cat rubbing its fur on your legs on a hot day.

He's assured of anonymity at this other store — and the prices there are cheaper. One of the reasons people still do stop at the general store is for the sociability, the predictable turns of phrase which vary only with the weather or the specifics of a calamity. The store down street is, in generic terms, not quite a supermarket but busy enough to honor silence at the cash register, not a surprise in the early 1970s, when even in this village Vermonters are just becoming used to taking on the odd job or two that brings them into contact with a public not common to the lives they lived on their farms and in the woods.

Israel does not come here more often than twice or three times a year, so what he buys from this store, interspersed with supplies from the bigger market, lasts him a long time. I don't see him walking by the gorge and the cemetery more than half a dozen times a year, but hermits stick out like sore thumbs where there's only one, and a person's right to privacy is easily invaded as other shadows pass back and forth behind starched curtains peering at this seldom-public soul.

Yes, there are other loners in this village, but they are not cut from the same cloth as this hermit. For example, when the ground thaws, Charlie Parker is commissioned to dig graves up there in the cemetery. He comes to the store. He's a bachelor who frequents school meetings, where, if you catch a glimpse of his busy pen on paper, he reveals a penchant for doodling tomb stones. He's also distinguished by the wicker shopping basket he carries on his arm from his house to the store and back. It's highly probable that the man tending the service station gas pumps one day when I stop for gas is also a bachelor, because how else is it possible to explain a level of dementia that caused him to lift the gas hose and nozzle between his legs and aim it — like a penis — at me?

A man who was a pillar of the East Poultney Church, who drove the school bus on which my children rode, was arrested for alleged child molestation some years after we had left the village. My girls used to play with one of his daughters at their house, and another daughter used to babysit for me. Only years later did I learn that my little sophisticates laughed off the bus driver's advances and those as well of a teenage babysitter who pulled his penis from his pants one evening. Only years later did I learn that one of my daughters witnessed a dead cat, hanged from a tree; a duck, dead because its leg froze in a pond; a coiled snake that demonstrated its wrath on a path ahead of my daughters. Only years later did I read of the tragedy of two teen lovers who hanged themselves together because the girl's father, our plumber, objected to their dating.

The fact that this loner, Israel, never talks, that for all intents and purposes he might as well not even have a name, gives him an importance, a role, almost as if a dignitary were stopping by. In other villages such a misanthrope might be mocked, for sometimes, it seems, the only way the public translates its own virtues is to juxtapose them against the blank corridors circumscribed by the scapegoat they can never understand. But here our hermit is honored and perhaps is a symbol, a shoring up for those who otherwise would choose this way to crumble, except that Israel yanks the mind back to reality because his world is too detached, too remote. He comes for brief moments and leaves his self-imposed isolation to co-mingle, if even silently. He inadvertently flatters those he chooses to patronize.

Does, in fact, the hermit have any duty to the village to which he belongs, other than that which he already performs, acting as a silent touchstone of some best-forgotten world?

His home is on past the gorge a mile or so, on a road called the Loop Road because you can enter the same road from two different spots off the main road. Here the valley widens just enough for some houses to scatter on one side; on the other are fields, separated and often flooded by the river.

Here, says a local historian, once was a settlement, a whole community with a company store. Floods came, though, and ravaged the narrow valley. A one-room schoolhouse is all that remains of any population center. The schoolhouse probably doesn't even go back as far as the flood, maybe only a hundred years, but it goes back long enough to have acquired an authentic patina of antiquity.

Here, then, in the schoolhouse, Israel Brown lives. The building that for some reason I always thought was yellow, perhaps by the way the light caught it, has the look of a not quite disreputable shanty, with nothing around the premises to give him away, not a sign of personality nor, for that matter, of life. This is simply a structure with an old outhouse, all covered over with synthetic shingles that appear to have once been red. Now faded, the color and locale give the building the distinction of being a frame of reference when folks ask for specific directions on the Loop Road.

By now, of course, it's hard to imagine that children might once have had anything to do with this small schoolhouse. The windows are boarded up with horizontal slabs that must shut out the light, but a few inches are left uncovered at the tops of the two windows facing the road, windows too high to look out of or into, affording just enough open space to let some sun come through. There's a chimney and, out back, facing the woods, a door and a small woodpile. Except for smoke from the chimney in the winter, the building gives every appearance of being abandoned.

Societies habitually make their citizens pay dues. The black house of medieval Scotland was a low-slung, windowless dwelling with only slits for doors. People were taxed according to the amount of light seeping in. Nobody boarded up the hermit's windows except presumably himself, levying a penance on himself that only society can inspire, secrets of a past that those who live in sunlight will never know.

One day when a neighbor is in the store, I ask her about the hermit.

She lives less than a quarter mile up the Loop Road, very near the schoolhouse. Once or twice a year, she tells me, a Cadillac with an out-of-state license plate parks by the schoolhouse. This is the arrival of the hermit's sister. The car hasn't been around for several years, however, and evidently this relative has stopped coming. As far as the neighbor knows, his only local contact is a kind person who occasionally brings him baked goods. Where he comes from, why he is here, why he lives alone, who he is, are unanswered questions.

What is he, then? Does he read? Is he a scholar sitting in the dingy building, searching for gold or truth as a medieval alchemist? Does he whittle? Is there an instrument so fine that his lack of commercial boldness will be a tragic loss to the music world? Does he paint? Or draw? Does he study the raccoons, the groundhogs and rabbits, the jays, sparrows and grosbeaks, the shifting seasons which move so unsubtly through Vermont?

Perhaps he is a self-styled Thoreau, unlucky to select his Walden too near a road for the privacy he needs for philosophical speculation; hence he boards up the windows to keep the curious away. Is he like Solzhenitsyn who, in another Vermont village, protected his privacy with high fences against snowmobiles and the public?

Is the hermit anything other than a man not old, not young, not so dirty but grimy from years of carrying coal in the loose-fitting jacket, woolen, tweed, worn with rather more style than the usual cast-off, carrying the heavy canvas bag of tinned meats?

This winter is a hard one, one of the coldest and snowiest on record, old timers say, although still not as ferocious, never could be, as the ones they remember from childhood.

One day, driving by the schoolhouse, I happen to think of the hermit, as the always-silent schoolhouse seems more vacant than before.

The neighbor tells me the hermit is in a bad way. He had gone to a nearby pond for water. He slipped in and got soaked up to the knees. A short while later, back at the schoolhouse, before he had time to get dry, he was chopping wood or shoveling snow or doing something physical and suffered a stroke. How long he lay alone in wet clothes in or outside near the schoolhouse, nobody knows. The mailman on the rural delivery route took Israel Brown's letters to the schoolhouse door and after pushing through the snow found the hermit alive, far from well, with severe frostbite.

When I last heard about him, he was an amputee, living in a nursing home somewhere in Rutland County.

As I drive by the schoolhouse, I look closely. Nothing is different. The windows are still boarded up; weeds grow high around the walls. But I've never noticed this before: The building that I have mistakenly always thought was yellow is mauve — a worn, muted, sad, almost gray and dingy color. But tell me, Israel Brown, how do I tell people who come to the store asking for directions to the Loop Road to turn left at your mauve-colored schoolhouse?

Stories of other local loners beg to be told. In a nearby village a woman was walking at midnight down the road, walking properly on the left-hand side, facing oncoming traffic, on the highway between Rutland and Pittsford. A friend and I stopped to pick her up. She settled in behind me in the Volkswagen. She was a women about my age, in her mid-thirties, not yet shopworn but distinctly sad.

At first we had gone right by her, had driven all the way to the swamp, in fact, where Tom stopped the car to light a cigarette, and where we watched the moon coming up through the cattails before we decided we should go back to get her.

She sat behind me on the edge of the seat, talking, nervous, and she pegged me as a teacher right away, although I'd not been in a classroom for years. Her voice was soft but strained. Her face had inexplicable sadness, but she was forced to be sociable because she found herself with two strangers in a Volkswagen, at midnight, on a dark country road. If she had been on a sidewalk outside a department store between Thanksgiving and Christmas, wearing a loose, dark coat and a bonnet tied under her chin, then I would have recognized her as she rang a Salvation Army bell. Or she might have been a nurse's aide, or a waitress serving mugs of coffee and pieces of pie à la mode on the late shift at a diner with linoleum and chrome decor.

There's only one place lit up in Pittsford late at night: the small country store. When we asked her where she was going and she couldn't tell us, our instinct was to drop her off at this store, where she could find a telephone and where there were lights. We stopped by the gas pump in front of the store. She thanked us. The last time I saw her that night she stood warily in the store's doorway, the glare detaining her from her adventure to nowhere.

A few days later, driving in my Volkswagen, I saw her again. This time the same woman was walking down a different road. She had stopped at the parapet of a bridge, where the water was swollen to spring proportions from rain and melting snow and ice. I didn't stop to pick her up. What sense does it make to give a woman a ride to somewhere when that isn't were she wants to go in the first place?

Only decades later did I discover how spot on I was then. Spring was nowhere on my horizon the Christmas after I made the final move to Vermont from New York. With perhaps more than a touch of SAD (seasonal affective disorder), I proceeded to top off whatever anti-anxiety meds I was taking with a glass of wine at a restaurant. As I grew more and more agitated, all celebratory demeanor collapsed. My daughters drove me to the emergency room of a local hospital, where I was supposed to spend the night. While they huddled with medical forces outside the examination room, I put on my coat and slipped out the hospital door. The stars were bright. The temperature hovered at minus-something. I was content marching in my Uggs down the road from Randolph to Barnard, past the hardware store and supermarket and onward. The police car snuck up behind me. I was escorted back to the hospital. My waiting family took me home.

East Poultney Cemetery

The greening of the graveyard is gradual,
a creeping of grass up the hill
from the lowest echelon ghost,
a slave to a captain in the Revolutionary War,
plodding slowly up the hill
past children's graves, tiny
interruptions between the blades
surrounding the Abigails and Sarahs
caught in their labors of sweet pain
before their time, then circling,
finally, the Calephs and Josiahs
who seeded this small patch
on a Poultney hill centuries ago.

The Library Inc.

My several-times-removed great-grandfather, John Reed Cobb, played his part with Ethan Allen and the Green Mountain Boys in helping to secure the territory that eventually became the State of Vermont. He fought in the Revolutionary War and doubtless sipped ale and hard cider with the Allen brothers and their cousin, Ebenezer Allen, who was one of the founders of Poultney and among my several-times-removed great uncles. They were known to frequent the Eagle Tavern, adjacent to the East Poultney General Store, which we owned. Only decades later did I learn that I was walking and living among ghosts of these forebears. The territory full of small towns west of the Connecticut River was held on behalf of England's King George III by Benning Wentworth, Royal Governor of New Hampshire. Wentworth had the authority to disburse the land. Like a piece of fabric, this territory was in dispute in 1768 because, it was being tugged and pulled between New York and New Hampshire. Who would own it? What is now Vermont became an independent republic in 1777. In 1791, this republic became the fourteenth state in the union.

Meanwhile, as of 1777, the grist mill at the Poultney River was grinding corn. The Eagle Tavern was built in 1780, and a few years later the Baptist Church sprang up. By 1823 Horace Greeley, founder of the *New York Tribune*, had moved into East Poultney. His house was occupied in the summer by a woman I dubbed Mrs. Horace Greeley. Whether she was related or not, I never knew. She would arrive in a big car in early summer. Her license plate read "Greeley." She left behind for the season her duties as housemother at a Champlain College dormitory in Burlington. Nobody but the liquor store owner down street in Poultney saw her during all those warm weeks.

George Jones lived on the village green too; he was a co-founder of the *New York Times*. Thus, this little village could claim not one but two founders of prominent New York daily newspapers.

The first library in Vermont took root here, supposedly where our barn was located near the store that dates to sometime in the 1830s. This historical fact was honored when my husband and I named the corporation we formed for the country store "The Library Inc." We liked the literary bent this brought to gallon jugs of pickled eggs that looked like eyeballs, sitting there by the old-fashioned cash register.

Across the road lived the family of a butcher, his wife and three teenagers. The daughter often babysat for us. One spring after the girls and I had been left to our own devices in East Poultney, our cat discovered a rabbit warren full of babies. There was a hole in the screen door into our apartment. Every morning for what seemed a week the cat leapt through this hole with yet another trophy dangling from its teeth. We were invaded by these tiny creatures. The cat chose to deposit its prey as far under the low-slung bunkbeds as possible, in a dark corner that could barely be reached by a broom. With effort and the broom I could sweep the baby of the day out from under the bed. Conditions varied. One bunny was alive enough and seemed healthy and it survived for a short while in a cardboard box, with my daughters lavishing it with attention while it breathed and tears when it died. Several were dead even before the broom brushed them out from under the bed. One was still alive but badly mangled. The girls carried this little blob of fur across the street and asked the butcher if he could please take care of it for us. Killing suffering rabbits was not a habit I chose to pursue.

On one side of us was the Eagle Tavern. An elegant old widow lived across the village green, in a house full of treasures someone in her family had collected on trips to the Orient. The mother of a runaway girl lived on the village green with her female companion. An artist who taught at Green Mountain College was mastering the creative art of wrapping dead animals in plastic for exhibitions. Another house belonged to a teacher and a football coach.

One neighbor had been a classmate of my mother's at Vassar. In the unspoken way that relationships have of becoming more than simple friendships, she nurtured me through some bleak times. Her husband was always hospitable, sometimes appearing at the door in his kilt, and known to pose nude for the art classes down at the college. He only had one eye because during a bout of depression he had gouged out the other. Frank predeceased Toni who, the last time I saw her, while I was visiting East Poultney, complained of a sore on her leg that wouldn't heal. Then I heard that she had been put in a nursing home because she had to have that abscessed leg amputated.

Over the bridge spanning a gorge lived a woman who dabbled in antiques and cared for an elderly duo across the Connecticut River in Hanover, New Hampshire. Her younger son was handsome. I vaguely remember there was an older brother.

Another family lived on a farm up the road. The mother's hospitality matched her kitchen, warm and effusive. Sadness crept in, however, when their only son committed suicide while attending the University of Vermont.

Other friends who had a brood of natural and adopted children were always up for sledding or skinny dipping. The mom wore bib overalls and smoked a corn cob pipe. Her husband gave me my first motorcycle ride.

In the apartment above the store, where we lived, my ball gowns from college and early marriage became dress-up costumes for my girls. Then came the day when these vestiges of what I thought my life would be wound up in the fireplace. I could no longer bear the burden of what might have been before my husband's mental illness descended on our family. Although dinner parties had been a staple of our life on Staten Island, with the exception of one large party we threw, we seldom indulged in candlelight — unless the power went out — while living above the East Poultney General Store.

Days of Mourning

Before the days of measuring and mourning it howled,
huddled by the fire we were warm,
knowing that this wind would pass.
Today we know it speeds in miles per hour
as we mark the passing of the storm
in gallons of oil and lost lives.

New York by Moped

Half my heart was in Vermont; the other half craved New York. I needed the Sunday fix that came with the *New York Times*. I subscribed to the *New Yorker*. As often as possible, I headed south with the girls. On one solo trip, after the girls and I were alone, I arranged to meet an old friend in the lobby of a Manhattan hotel from where, presumably, we would take the elevator to his room. Several cups of coffee later in the hotel café, what might have become a dalliance was stopped in its tracks. Although we suspected our spouses were in the habit of cooing to each other, neither of us wanted any more complications in our lives. When we were still innocents, the fun and laughter of our Italy days were shadows mocking our responsibilities. I limped back to friends on Staten Island. When my host opened the door, I sobbed on his shoulder.

On another visit I championed the Moped.

New York by Moped. I am vulnerable to a whole new world: to purse snatchings, taxi cabs, manhole covers, exhaust fumes and, above all, the magic of the city in June, or probably any other month, for that matter. I am so vulnerable to this magic that I may, in fact, fall in love — irrevocably, irrationally and joyfully — with an imported creature with a strange name: Moped.

The following is a synopsis of such a romantic encounter. As is more often than not in an affair of the heart, this encounter was serendipitous, unresolved and unnerving. But then, whoever said that the course of true love with a Moped would ever run smooth?

This piece manifests my own mania, or, perhaps, euphoria at being unshackled by duties at the country store. I remember writing all of this down swiftly in order to capture the joy of a new experience and, perhaps, a little bit of risk.

Chapter I. The Staten Island Ferry. Something in the early summer (mid-June) air whetted the urge for adventure. First there was the man selling tickets to the Staten Island Ferry. He saw my Vermont license plate and said that he had been to New Hampshire once and got a speeding ticket. He had paid the $15 fine, and they sent him back $10. I told him if he'd gone faster, maybe he'd have made money on the ticket.

I tried to find the line of the cars boarding the ferry on the Manhattan side. A boat had just left and so had all the lines. Confused, I drove from one slip to the next, with people yelling at me to get back in line. What line? A kindly white-haired gentleman, very gallant, took the time to explain patiently that if I went back onto the island I would find the line. This meant coming by the ticket window again, and seeing me, my ticket friend look surprised to find me back so soon. I found two cars by now parked in a line and got behind them. The nice white-haired gentleman came out of his way to my car window and was terribly pleased his directions had taken so well. He tipped his beret and walked on.

Chapter II. Vanities. My Staten Island hosts and I relived a substantial part of our lives at *Vanities*, an off-Broadway comedy (circa 1976–1980), where enough people laugh to give the impression that cheer-leading is indeed one of the universals of contemporary American society.

Chapter III. The Father. Host father stays home Sunday to play tennis and make sure his children — and mine — are having a good time. Hostess, who I forgot to mention is a Texas girl, thereby providing personal insight into *Vanities*, and guest, who has made the ferry passage, plan a let-it-happen kind of day shopping on the Lower East Side and having dinner later with a friend on West 20th. We will travel by — wait and see.

We walk to the garage, a fortress of padlocks and bolts. Three combinations later, a heavy gate is lifted. Inside: a half-dozen bikes. Sitting shyly in the corner, tethered to the wall, the quiet, gentle, unpretentious Moped, blue, bound by chain and padlock, proudly equipped with black, simulated-leather panniers, waiting to be freed, to move out into the Staten Island air. Hostess wheels Moped out gently. We close the garage doors, bolt and padlock them. Moped is charged. Hostess is in the driver's seat. I'm perched behind, knuckles white, clutching the back of the seat with a large straw purse over one arm. (Note the purse, an object of interest later in this story.) Two mothers, with five children between us, we begin a journey on what may in the real world be the closest thing to a flying carpet.

Chapter IV. The Journey. Hostess explains there are no rules for Moped except those which apply to bikes. Knuckles still white, we whiz down the cobblestones of Staten Island and catch the 12 o'clock ferry, standing on the lower deck within hailing distance of Moped, for already I can't let it out of my sight.

Judging from the comments and attention elicited at every red light and street corner, Moped in June is a novelty, or at least Moped in June with two mamas is a novelty. (If we had filled the panniers with Moped brochures, we could have converted at least a score of people in one easy ride through lower Manhattan.)

We stop at South Street Seaport and prepare to tether Moped to a light pole in front of the shrimp cocktail vendor who hastens to our side explaining that objects tethered to light poles — including Mopeds — have been known to disappear and that we ought to stable it in his garage, right behind his table of shrimp cocktails. We agree, then purchase two paper cups of shrimp cocktail and munch our way through the market and museums along the waterfront.

Chapter V. Lonely for Moped. We return, explain to the shrimp cocktail vendor's young son the cost and economy of our friend, discuss the relative merits of various tethering devices (for example, chains and padlocks with which to secure the creature) and, waving goodbye, head up through Chinatown. Before we reach Chinatown, however, we catch the attention of a cluster of nuns in traditional habit, sporting yellow balloons in honor of Gay Pride Day. One nun steps up to Moped and gifts us with a balloon. This festoons Moped until it pops.

On the way to Chinatown, I know my future lies with Moped, romantically and economically. Why not take advantage of Mopedphilia (Moped mania)? Imagine shocking pink, chartreuse and lemon-yellow Moped costumes, durable to withstand weather, billowing to catch the breeze, like sails, down city streets. Banners: Don't mind me, I'm Moped. Or: Eat your heart out, you, I'm Moped. Ain't it marvelous? It's a Moped. There could be Moped bars and Mopedwiches, Moped sneakers, Moped munchies.

All right, enough already, says my friend. Furthermore, I say, someone should write a book about how to live your life when you discover you're a Moped maniac.

Marvelous Moped, I croon, marvelous Moped. The influence of *Vanities* and the cheerleading syndrome hung over from last night bolster a quick check for Moped teams, rallies, Moped gymkhanas, exhibitions of Moped drivers.

The least you can do, I say, is get a bunch of Moped brochures from your leader and tell him you'll hand them out as you travel along. And in return he will give you, absolutely free, another Moped, for you could be the Fuller Brush persona of Moped. And the truth is that, judging by all the people who ask us questions in the space of four hours, we probably scored leads — even without brochures — that the Moped marketing department can track. I say I'll ghostwrite the brochure and for my cut receive a new Moped. Only I want a red one.

So my friend and hostess concurs that this might be a way to get ready money and I've just decided to give up my bucolic life in the oh-so-green hills of Vermont and move to Manhattan and ride a Moped and get rich quick writing *The Diary of a Moped Freak*, which can only be paralleled in literary potential by *The History of Tom Jones, a Foundling* or *Moll Flanders*.

Chapter VI. Hallucinations. When all of a sudden I start seeing things I've never seen before: buildings where up to the height of at least six floors, about as high as the neck can bend, are arrays of embellishments I'd only observed once before. This was while I was riding an elephant through Manhattan, at the preview of the upcoming Barnum & Bailey Circus. I became intimate for the duration of the ride with occupants living several stories up. The abundance of flourishes teases the eye to find any conformity at all. There are enormous displays of chiaroscuro — all in brick, with smokestacks thrown in and touches of faded blue shutters singing on broken hinges and geraniums that never looked so red in the country and fire escapes rampant, placed like notes on a piece of sheet music.

I continue in this euphoric state all day, my mood only potentially dented when riding back home on a southerly route through the Bowery. Here an entourage, perhaps five or six strong, of motorcycle-mounted dudes, Hells Angels, perhaps, swarm Moped and attempted to jerk straw purse off of my arm. We foil this attempt. They fail. Moped then charges dutifully on toward the Staten Island Ferry and I make my way back to East Poultney.

To Bella, Gloria, et al.

As I was sitting home at ease
the bras were burning wildly.
When women's lib was at its peak,
I viewed it only mildly.
But now I'm looking for a job,
a change from hibernation,
and want to thank you for your work
while I've been on vacation.

Dark Days

Despite forays to New York for pleasure, and later for work, Vermont was the magnet that always pulled me back. Years passed. I was well into my sixties before I could see a family with young children playing together without immediately tearing up. I mourned the loss of family, which by my definition included a husband and father. While in Italy I had witnessed some things that became pivotal to the rest of my life — the huge love Italians have for their families and the ways they treat their children. I don't think I mourned the absence of my husband. The mentally ill person he had become differed night and day from the man I had married. For the children, however, I felt it was important that he be in their lives whenever he chose to resurface. He and the woman who would be his second wife were invited to our Christmas one year in East Poultney, soon after we divorced. He brought gifts for the girls and for this woman. I watched her open several packages, including one containing a leather jacket. Under the tree there was nothing for me.

I think this was the Christmas my youngest requested a bathrobe. I went to a fabric store. But what was I thinking? Or did she pick out the fabric, with me oblivious to what the repercussions of her choice would be? The fluffy exterior was a lovely wine color. But the inside was scratchy and brown. This was not material for clothing but was yardage for a toilet-seat cover or bath mat. Although I broke several sewing machine needles as I stitched away, I don't recall that it ever crossed my mind that the fabric was wrong. Mentally, I was in some other world. The garment was presented on time. The first try-on destined the robe to oblivion, but not before it entered the tapestry of family lore as a prime piece of embroidery.

Now officially a single parent, I gave no thought to trying to get child support from a man who was barely holding himself together. My confidence as a wage earner and a professional expanded as editorial and public relations assignments came effortlessly. These positions led me back and forth between Vermont and New York. I always wondered why a simple and engaging toy, a Duncan yo-yo, shared my maiden name, Duncan. This clan's motto is "Learn to Suffer."

I was learning how to juggle the household duties by myself. My husband was no longer barraging me with his tangential theories. My mind was relaxed because by now, having followed the advice of a doctor and authority figure, I was addicted to Valium. I wasn't crying; I wasn't laughing. Instead I was numb. I did whatever was called for to get through coming home from work, preparing dinner and spending time with the girls. As often as not dinner was roasted chicken served with peas and rice. This menu was easy to prepare, and everybody ate it without complaints.

Did I read good-night stories to them then? I can't remember. Did I accidentally wash fiberglass curtains with the family clothing? Everyone remembers, especially my child who was then a first-grader. She had been invited to a friend's house after school. When I picked her up, she told me the friend's mother had given her a bath and fresh clothes because she was itching so badly from her own fiberglass curtain–infected garments. This became yet another stitch in the family embroidery.

Evenings I was moonlighting, freelance writing. As I sat at the dining room table in front of the old Royal (manual) typewriter, I would remind the children: "Please be quiet. Mommy's bringing home the bacon." And there were lists of daily chores that I expected the girls would pay attention to before I came home. Only later did I learn that these lists gave the older child power as she ordered the younger to perform, setting up a dysfunctional relationship between two sisters.

Meanwhile, other relationships were emerging after the divorce. My one-time husband eventually married the woman who visited at Christmas. In turn she, while in wedlock, fell in love with a male professor. This severed her marriage. Her relationship with the professor evolved with revelations that he had long felt he was actually a woman, and that *he* needed to become a *she*. I am not sure that the concept of transexual was in the vernacular at this time. I had never heard of it. At any rate, the complicated thinking manifested by mental illness paled in comparison to this new reality of assorted genders.

Any expectations — about almost everything — that I may have harbored had sunk under the need to secure money for myself and my two daughters. I could not even afford the expectation that my car would start, because too many times it didn't, once resulting in a one-way trip to the car repair shop to pick up my distressed auto. I flagged a ride from East Poultney to wherever the garage was with two strange men. As the miles clicked away, I became increasingly nervous, and then I heard the automatic lock fasten the back-seat doors. I didn't even expect to get safely to the auto shop.

Years later the teacher of a memoir class asked us to focus on expectations. On the way home I found myself pulling the car to the side of the road to write down my thoughts on expectations. Maybe people who have never had rugs pulled out from under them can hang on to expectations or belief systems or assumptions. Strangely, I can't. What this means for me is erasing all conditionals from thinking and vocabulary and boring into the reality of the moment — or into my reality of the moment. I have no anticipation of *will* or *won't*; rather, I am just relieved when something goes right.

Unbeknownst to me, I was learning the lesson May Sarton explored in her book *Journal of a Solitude*, revealing differences between being lonely and being alone. Although from childhood I never lacked for perseverance, a newfound grit cast any tendencies toward procrastination into the shadows, along with an emotional life that I unconsciously perceived as being superfluous and a luxury. After all, in my own family of origin I was the one who ran away from family arguments at the dinner table. I had no emotional patterning to fall back on, other than that of anger. I was simply, numbly putting one foot in front of the other, some nights standing naked in front of the floor-length mirror in my frostbitten bedroom, wondering at what reflected back as a waste of resources and most certainly missed opportunities. I never defined myself by the many roles I picked up like pairs of knitting needles. The roles were simply means to ends, strategies to care for my daughters, to put food on the table and to pay the mortgage. Did the roles dangle any appendage of self-worth over me as I moved in and out of them? No. Because there was no self-worth, only numbness. Buried somewhere very deep was the suspicion that I was the only person who was ever going to take care of my emotional needs.

Feminism in the 1970s ran wantonly through Vermont's Green Mountains. Women embraced stridency and lesbianism. Women were given a perceived "power" of filling our own gas tanks as full-service gas stations disappeared. Filling my own tank for the first time, I called out to another woman who was similarly engaged. "See what women's lib has done for us?" Because Vermont is a tight community, instinct warned me to stay away from this movement of angry women. However, I did cherry pick the foment, writing an op-ed piece for the *Barre-Montpelier Times-Argus* on pay discrepancies between women and men in the same jobs. At this time, in the mid-1970s, women made sixty-six cents on the man's dollar. The needle is still droning its way to this seemingly unachievable finish line of equality.

One summer day when the girls were visiting their father in Ohio, or maybe they had gone to the mansion on a lake in Canada that his second wife's father owned, I decided to make a cultural foray to Boston. A neighbor and I went. For budgetary reasons we chose to stay in a YWCA — sharing one bed and a dorm-style bathroom. On this occasion I vowed that never again would borderline poverty mandate lying in bed with a woman. Perhaps there are results when we call out what we need to the Universe. Unbeknownst to me then, I would soon begin enjoying bed linen thread counts reaching the stratosphere, in suites with walls swathed in silk and with adjacent private baths displaying hand-milled soaps and Turkish towels.

You Betcha

I'm glad that life's knocked me about
so I might learn to laugh and shout,
instead of paling in the dusk,
a thwarted, proper, timid husk.

Moving On

My daughters and I still lived in the apartment over the store in East Poultney. I hired a store manager to cover during my return to journalism, which was soon followed by a foray into the world of radio, a path that eventually wound to a public relations position at a ski resort. A Rutland radio station hired me for a short time in an on-air position. I was to present an energetic and spirited community through the radio. My job was to source various community groups and charities and invite their spokespeople to the station to tell their stories on-air. I was the interviewer. The Peppermint Pipers sent in such a swell of nurses to sing one morning that the station manager had to be called in to find out what was going on in his studio. The fire marshal would not have approved. Showcasing the vibrancy of the community on-air helped the station draw more advertisers — and listeners.

A small weekly newspaper called *The Resorter* was designed to appeal — and sell — to tourists flocking to Lake St. Catherine, Lake Bomoseen and Lake Dunmore, all near Rutland. I was hired to take charge of the paper. Someone else owned it. My mandate was to sell advertising, collect the monies, create stories and photos of interesting places to visit and then deliver the newspaper. I asked a neighbor to write a cooking column. A professor at Castleton State College (now University) wrote a weekly column on the geology of the region. *The Resorter* and WSYB radio put my name out in the greater community. Someone referred me to what would be my new workday home, the ski resort where I was invited to serve as News Bureau Director. The mountain was an hour commute from East Poultney. The driving time fluctuated from an hour to what could become many minutes more, depending on how hard the snow was falling. The good news was that my daughters could come to the mountain and ski for free on weekends, while I worked. They both became fine skiers.

I have always been a good foot soldier in my positions. At the mountain I learned about and became a practitioner of public relations from the ground up, drawing attention to these mountains and welcoming ski writers who, like restaurant reviewers, arrived to assess ski conditions for their audiences.

Interesting people surfaced. Although I never had the opportunity to meet him, I have a warm, hand-written note from Lowell Thomas sending his regrets that he could not attend a function to which I'd invited him. Archer Winston was the reclusive movie reviewer and ski writer for the *New York Post* who wrote me a kind letter. At a function for restaurateurs held in Rutland, Vermont, I met Skitch Henderson, who was still the musical conductor for *The Tonight Show Starring Johnny Carson*. When someone at this gathering asked me how I liked my Scotch, I quipped: "Straight, like I like my men." Skitch apparently took a shine to me and invited me to dine with him at his house in Stowe. But I did my homework. I knew he was married and had a reputation as a womanizer. I declined. Later on in New York, one man with the loveliest blue eyes I've ever seen suggested after a business meeting at his office that he would like to see me again. This aging actor (and perhaps a roué) was Douglas Fairbanks Jr. Proximity to the world of celebrities intrigued me. Later I would assist with the promotional needs of the late Bobby Short, who cast his vocal magic at the Carlyle, a repository of the rich and famous.

A colleague and I created a radio series that aired locally. This was an innovative approach to public relations outreach. Our shows were dubbed by the resort's marketing director as the "ding-dong tapes," his reflection on the authors — not the content. Before the days of desktop computers, my copy for press releases was hand typed, submitted for review and, if mistake-free, channeled to the mailroom for duplicating and posting. Should an error creep through, it was my face that wore the egg, as I was required to roll up my sleeves to unstuff and restuff the envelopes while facing the stares and glares of unhappy mailroom staffers, who were no-nonsense women.

One day, however, I was ordered to become part of the ex officio team — all women — who daily subbed at the switchboard so that the regularly assigned switchboard operator could take a lunch break. This stuck in my craw, as I perceived that I was now placed in the pool of secretaries and other female assistants. On my first and only day at this duty, I failed to pass muster at the switchboard and was never called upon to do this again. Did I employ guerrilla tactics? Maybe.

I began learning the business of business in an environment where the ski season is as evanescent as snowflakes. Money was to be made between October/November and April, with May extensions for publicity's sake. Years later, when I consulted for Miramax Films, the urgency of the promotional moment was even more profound, as box office revenues were measured over a few weeks.

Basically I had carte blanche to create and fulfill ideas that would bring positive visibility to the ski resort. The ideas were probably not profound, but my energy level was, and I loved stirring the pot.

One weekend, however, I was asked to keep silent about goings-on at the mountain. It was the culmination of President's Week, which traditionally draws many families to the mountain. A colleague with a subversive bent that bordered on anarchy had recently been spending time with a Manhattan woman who was, according to him, an evolving political revolutionary. Perhaps it was Friday morning when a strange message was found on a ski slope, warning of an explosive device that had been placed in a ski locker at a base lodge. Soon other notes were found. Police were called and, indeed, a non-detonating, incendiary device was discovered in a ski locker. Before this incident I had seen on this colleague's desk in his apartment the ingredients for making such a device. Coincidence? I don't think so. Doubtless he took a high level of satisfaction at watching his superiors on the busiest weekend of the year skiing in circles while keeping the mountain and facilities open despite the explosive threat. After the weekend I reported to one of the vice presidents what I had seen on my colleague's desk. He told me to report it to the state police, which I did. Decades later I learned that this "case" had never been solved.

That public relations was on the periphery of a corporate world was my perception after working for three ski resorts. These were worlds that, right after Vietnam, were peopled with young men who had seen action and who now used the mountains as places where they could begin to heal, far away from the mainstream world. It was easier to do battle with a blizzard on a steep slope and be part of a crew of snowmaking cowboys than it was to don suit and tie in an urban setting. But this didn't make these worlds any less corporate, particularly when I witnessed paper shredders in action, cancelling out hard-fought corporate secrets in the highly competitive environment of the New England ski world. Meanwhile, the youthful, testosterone-driven staff surveyed snow depths hourly, measuring and reporting their findings more frequently than a parent assesses the temperature of a sick child.

At this time in this snow-driven world, women played supporting roles to the men who daily donned the ski world's version of mail and armor for protection against inclement conditions. The Broadway show *Camelot* was still popular and it took only a sip of wine to bring the authors of the ding-dong tapes to giggles as we envisioned the males of the mountain creating conditions Lerner and Loewe would understand:

> *It's true! It's true! The crown has made it clear.*
> *The climate must be perfect all the year …*
> *And there's a legal limit to the snow here*
> *In Camelot.*

The weather could be either friend or foe and with the weather rose and fell the fortunes of the corporation. These knights weren't on horseback but on snowmobiles. They were armed with snow-machine guns instead of jousting lances. Although the damsels awaiting them at the castle didn't stand up and cheer, there was admiration aplenty upon their return to ponder over spreadsheets behind closed office doors.

Five years after setting foot on this mountain, I left. This was not a happy occasion for me, but it surely was for another colleague in the marketing department who was assigned to supervise me while I cleared my desk. He advised, "We're glad to be rid of you and your crazy ideas." He must have been thinking of the ding-dong tapes. Sadly, my children were in the office when I was ordered to vacate. What occasioned this debacle was my reaction to being asked to do something that I thought to be patently dishonest. This story tells it all. This story also represents the transition from the good girl who always did as people said I should. This time, although I obeyed, I also rebelled.

Christmas week loomed, but there was little to no natural snow on the ground in Vermont. The science of snowmaking was still in its infancy. The snowmakers had laid down a narrow strip of machine-made snow on the ski slope that beginners used. The marketing director ordered me to report to my media contacts that for those ski-and-vacation hungry masses, skiing for the upcoming holidays was alive and well. The rest is history.

The mountain anticipated skiers in the thousands. If word did not get out, the number could drop to four hundred. The pressure was on me from the director of marketing and the head of the company to persuade the ski press that ski conditions were alive and well, without divulging that "alive and well" meant a narrow strip of machine-made snow. Ski conditions were lousy all over Vermont. In response to my reluctance to relay the corporate spin, I was told I that if I didn't make the calls, I would not have a job and that I should go home and think about it.

With this humiliation under my belt, I made a vow to myself. Under no circumstances, at any time, was I ever going to perform a task that goes against my best judgment. A goal of a public relations campaign is to sway public opinion. However, deception should never be part of the task of persuasion. I had earned the trust of ski journalists. I valued their trust. Gathering advice from colleagues, I did come up with a strategy that satisfied the corporate mandate and did not compromise the facts of the situation. Perhaps it was anger that inspired me eventually to come up with messaging I was comfortable with and that I delivered in time to save the season and my neck.

My story served three purposes: to alleviate out-of-state fears that Vermont skiing was shut down for lack of snow; to restore faith internally among Vermonters that the ski industry was working its tail off for all of us; to serve as a tool in showing the level of professionalism and concern the ski industry had regarding its responsibility to the state economy.

After completing my mission, I wrote a letter to my boss, the marketing director, outlining in no uncertain terms what it felt like to work under the threat of being fired. I asked that the letter be put in my personnel file. This missive to the marketing department was followed by another memo I wrote on January 1, 1980, to the president of the ski resort company. This second letter was a response to the president, who requested that I remove my first letter from my personnel file and apologize to the marketing director, promising that "things would be better than ever" after I had complied. What "better" meant, I could not foresee. And I would not apologize.

This was part of my response to the president:

… I have no desire to be anyone's scapegoat in this matter, to have people tell me that "I responded because my back was up against the wall" or that my lack of response or not making the calls on two given days is "a very big mistake…" that ultimately feeds back to me. These are responses I have heard from two persons, responses which, in my call to you, I hoped, in deference to points of view and differences thereof and out of a strong belief that "I disagree with what you say but defend to death your right to say it" still holds some sway in a rational world you might help curtail.

Because I do not feel, nor will I ever feel that I owe an apology for placing the memo in my personnel file, and because I feel that ultimately more harm than good comes from not dealing with reality, I understand that I am placing you in an untenable position and, therefore, in order to spare anyone further embarrassment, I request termination of employment effective two weeks from now, or immediately if you wish.

I am not unhappy here. I have enjoyed the privilege of working for the company, the privilege of getting to know some very fine people. I appreciate the opportunities and privileges the corporation has afforded me.

In retrospect, was my anger against the marketing director or against a machine called Sara that was out of control? He and I had had our differences. Once he told me I gave him a headache. I retorted that he gave me a stomachache. We had a kind of Mexican stand-off relationship. I don't think I was constituted to acknowledge him as boss and myself as underling. Rather, my view was of peer to peer. Years later I've wondered how he coped with the evening that the mountain entertained VIPs and journalists visiting for Olympic activities preceding the games at Lake Placid. I was charged with seating arrangements for the press, including a large contingent from Japan who tendered their cameras only while wearing white gloves and who didn't speak a word of English. I assigned my boss to host their table. He didn't like small talk. Maybe he was relieved.

After Salem (and Arthur Miller)

We are what we always were but naked now.
Gutted, drained, stripped away the garden that was our home,
faring farther than our minds dare range
to the plastic, non-biodegradable wasteland of our poppets,
perpetuating in our folly Salem naked,
and the wind, God's icy wind, will blow.
Stripped from the coal mine, drained from the rich soil,
gutted from the rivers and the seas,
we have gorged unto death our dignity
on this miscreant, greed,
lead to view its virtues,
dancing, naked
in the moonstruck Salem wood,
as self-appointed, stiff-necked clerics
sanctify acquisitions as our noble end,
instead of pewter, gold,
to shed light on the altar of our desperate faith,
substantiating missiles for the gifts of self,
heeding, surely, as the citizens of Salem
long ago, addiction to sublime goals.
We are what we always were but naked now,
and the wind, God's icy wind, will blow.

Black and White

I continued to live in my own black-and-white world. I was oblivious to realities around me, secure in my ability to type and think and therefore to be employable, and secure in my ability to support myself and my children, for whom I alone was responsible.

Within weeks of the ski resort debacle, I moved our household from East Poultney to New York City to take a position as a city reporter at United Press International (UPI), a news organization that was housed in the *New York Daily News* building on 42nd Street. This position was short-lived, possibly because I was reluctant to leave my sleeping children alone in our Staten Island apartment so I could report on an early morning chemical fire in New Jersey, or perhaps because I brought scant interest one long summer day to a pair of show-offs trying to scale the calves of the Statue of Liberty. My assignment was to report on the duo's ascent up the maiden and to find out why they were doing this. They were up there and I was down below so I was unable to ask the questions needed to create a story. Weekday assignments were always press-release driven. This means that a company or a cause sent a missive to the UPI desk advising of news and/or an activity at such and such a time on such-and-such a date. This would provide fodder for the insatiable appetite of wire service news. One event that may have been related to nuclear energy was staged on a sidewalk with a handful of protestors lying down on the cement and kicking the air. I had no curiosity or interest in these shenanigans. I was not cynical enough to be a good street reporter.

Out-of-office assignments usually found me walking back down 42nd Street or Lexington Avenue at lunchtime, absolutely the worst time to stride with speed and always an exercise in zigging and zagging. Sometimes the press conference was held in tandem with an elegant lunch. I might have been invited, but the wire service frowned on reporters accepting these invitations. Was I perhaps striding back to the office trying to digest humble pie?

Two stories stand out to this day. I was assigned to speak with a daughter of Roman Totenberg, whose priceless Stradivarius violin had been stolen. Nearly four decades would pass before the violin was returned to the family. I don't remember exactly where the interview took place, but I remember the ambiance. Overlooking the street were panes of windows casting muted light into what felt like an atelier in Paris. It's possible that UPI (and my work) broke this story of loss, a story that later would turn out to be a story of betrayal. One of Mr. Totenberg's music students had stolen the instrument.

Another story concerned a slice of Manhattan geography known as Rikers Island, the city's prison, which was surrounded by a very large moat. I picked up the phone one afternoon for City Desk and was told that a prisoner was on the lam and swimming his way to freedom. I hung up the phone and told the editor. He asked me which direction the escapee was swimming. As I was clueless, the story went to another journalist.

Clearly my forte lies with music — not with mobsters and weirdos. My genetic code recoils at skepticism, relying rather on the belief that honesty prevails.

Sustaining a life in Manhattan requires energy. I was out of sync with the city; my heart lay elsewhere. Whatever phase of daze I was now in led me back to Vermont and into the arms of a waiting lover with whom I would share a household for more years than were healthy for either of us. Everything I owned went into purchasing the house we shared in Montpelier. He provided for monthly living expenses. I was unwilling to burden him with the expenses of my daughters. I worked — too much — to pay the bills.

Some of the bills were credit card charges carried north from New York. One card, in fact, disappeared. I couldn't pay the monthly balance that was required after treating my children to *Annie* and *Oklahoma*. These evenings on Broadway had helped lessen the impacts of other issues, such as one daughter's broken leg, sustained when she fell twenty-five feet from a tree in a neighbor's yard. A pleasant-seeming man I'd met had invited me for a drink after work. Somehow I was confused about where we were to meet — this was before cell phones — so the drink didn't happen. To this day I regret that he probably thought I blew him off. But when I returned home, both girls were sitting with my friend of Moped fame on our living room couch. She had come to our aid in a serious emergency. They were waiting for me to take my daughter to the hospital, where she then spent one week confined to her hospital bed with a broken leg. Her bone healed. My guilt didn't.

> Ladybug! Ladybug! Fly away home.
> Your house is on fire
> And your children all gone.

Was her broken leg a quid pro quo because I was a wee bit late getting home?

I think the Broadway shows were an attempt to assuage everything that was going wrong. This included the reality that I missed a man in Vermont who was unable to give me my space, who called me and came to visit and who was weeping when he picked me up at the *Daily News* building. The tears had their intended effect, and I prepared to move back to Vermont with the girls, to live with him in Montpelier.

The Old Man

Last night there was an old man in my dreams
who desired my hand to guide him
down roads blown by the salt wind,
and I minded the chore of moving him to the sea,
both dragging our feet
through the truculent, seaweed shore.

Just Call Joe

The relationships that I depended on in these early days of being single were male. Today I have a wonderful network of female friends with whom phone chats, white wine in hand, are always welcome. For a time most of the men I knew were named Joe. One was the lawyer who drew up my divorce papers. After learning that my children's father was paying no child support, this lawyer was able to secure in my name, as the sole head of household, the house in Portland, Oregon, a property that my former husband and I had held jointly. When this property finally sold, I finally had some breathing room. I later learned that my former husband accumulated savings that he kept secret during our marriage. We were both scrambling.

Another Joe was my mechanic. I had a penchant for Saabs, all second-hand, and these finicky, cult automobiles were always in and out of his shop.

I was wooed from Manhattan back to Vermont by yet another Joe, a powerful man on the lobbying scene in Vermont with whom I had been conducting an on-and-off-again affair and against whom my better judgment held no sway. This time my daughters and I were living in Montpelier, Vermont, in what my New York friends dubbed an executive house that we shared with Joe, who became my live-in mate. Months into this arrangement Joe announced that his divorce was to be final. All the while I thought he was already newly single. I purchased our house by using any savings I had accrued and cashing in insurance policies. This house was not my first choice; but Joe — who was a rising star in the art of influencing state politicos related to what was fast becoming its most important industry, skiing — determined that the much-less-expensive farmhouse outside of town that I preferred wasn't suited to his entertaining needs. We were going to live together. He would pay the taxes, utilities, maintenance and the day-to-day living expenses for what was now a family of four. He had steered into young adulthood his own four children from his previous marriage. I reasoned that it would be unfair of me to burden him with expenses for two more children.

Work fell into my lap, including a stint as lifestyle and business editor on the *Barre-Montpelier Times-Argus*, working under Bill Porter, a fine mentor. I churned out copy and laid out pages of the kinds of news that people clip for scrapbooks and posterity. I loved every minute of my time at the newspaper until Bill left and his replacement assigned me, in addition to normal duties, all of the advertising specials. These were mini newspapers in and of themselves for which I was expected to produce original — not canned — copy on a regular basis.

Afternoons, after working at the newspaper, I drove to a nearby ski resort. Here I put on the hat of public relations maven for several hours, coming home long after the girls had returned from school. Weekends I went back up to the ski mountain. Any free time often found me at my home desk, writing for several magazines and a business journal. Work must have fatigued me. Whether from the children or from Joe, conflict and stress placed burdens on me that I did not have the energy to shoulder. I suspect I just took a Valium.

After years of having the world on my shoulders, I longed for peace and times when I could breathe deeply, safely. While still in East Poultney I had sought help from a mental health practitioner in Rutland. His name was also Joe. Upon meeting me this Joe asked if he could tape our sessions. I said no. What I did do for as long as I was in his office was cry. I became bored and restless hearing myself repeat painful stories. I watched a box of tissues dwindle as I sobbed after exhorting that I felt as if I had lost the steel rod that was holding me together. Two sessions and a wastebasket full of soggy tissues later, I concluded this therapy. When stripped from what then were the sum of my parts – my husband, my marriage, my family of origin, my community, my friends, my church fellowship – the center refused to hold.

In hindsight, therapy might have prompted me to recognize what was dearest to me, my sense of being in control. I thought I knew what I needed, and that was to be in an emotionally safe place with another person, failing to understand that I had to be in my own safe place before that could happen. (One family member who read this manuscript early on reflected: "What do I think about this woman? I think she is an obstinate coot who may have oppositional defiance disorder and who is very alone.")

Still on the lookout for the proverbial safe port, I imposed this need for a safe place on the new partnership with my lover Joe. The relationship was far from supportive. I rushed home from the newspaper and the ski resort before Joe got home to make sure the girls' beds were made. If the beds weren't made, he put pressure on me to get them to toe the line. Stacking wood and shoveling snow that may have been jolly family projects from his past became stress points if the girls weren't right there to pitch in. He didn't realize that the girls and I had managed our own house, perhaps by fits and starts, with daily written lists they could tackle before I returned from work. Now the chores were being assigned by someone else, and the girls didn't welcome them.

We didn't use the front door accessing the main floor of this split-level home but entered via the door through the garage, where a short staircase led up to the main floor and another staircase descended to a subterranean level that housed a ping-pong table and a newly installed coal bin. Coal would supply the cheapest energy, according to Joe. He was footing the energy bills at a time when the only emissions anyone ever considered were those from an idling engine in a closed garage. Another short staircase off the main floor led up to three bedrooms and a bath; and yet another short flight of stairs led to a small study and the master bedroom, with spacious, to-die-for his and hers closets. There was even a trash compactor in the kitchen.

Everything had been thought out. One exception was the wall-to-wall carpeting that clung like moss over all the stairs and throughout the corridors and rooms. I had always disliked such carpeting that now was a major feature of my new life as the parvenu of a star lobbyist in a small state capital.

Decades later my youngest daughter shared with me a scene of which I have no recollection. I cannot remember taking a bag of what she said was cat food and methodically dispensing pellets over the carpet-clad floors throughout the house. This, of course, had to be vacuumed. My daughter remembers vacuuming for what to her seemed hours.

Evidently a young friend of my daughter's witnessed the benediction by cat food and asked her: "Is your mother okay?"

I was not. But recently, while trying to combat an aspersion as to my sanity, I researched the merits of clay-based cat litter for purposes other than the litter box. The disbursing of whatever it actually was wasn't a symptom of mental stress, even though I didn't know how ill I must have been. I was not out of line. The cat litter would, indeed, absorb smells and moisture. The cat litter did not, however, slow down the growth of mushrooms that sprung up in the carpet of the garage-level office where I worked after working all day. The mushrooms appeared when the garage and basement flooded. Rather than being disturbing presences, they rather intrigued me. This review of a past action, dispensing cat litter, comes as a particular relief, for within a short period of time after conducting this bizarre carpet cleaning, I was hospitalized for ingesting too much Valium.

What were the triggers of this episode? Driving into the garage and hitting the wrong button to automate the door, thus bringing the door down on top of the car? Coming home one night with my daughters to find our living room taken over by legislators — perhaps a dozen or more — being hosted by lobbyist Joe? This scene wasn't stressful, but as I cordially stood by Joe at the door saying good night as they were leaving, not one of them acknowledged my presence. Perhaps the trigger was arriving home from work late on the afternoon of my birthday and giving the car an early spring bath, only to find myself locked out of my house for several hours on a cold April night until Joe came returned, without birthday greetings. I did anything Joe asked me to do, including dipping into my savings account to purchase a mink coat that he fancied I should have. The savings account was attacked on another occasion when an Oriental rug company came to Montpelier and Joe determined that our living room needed a new carpet. How I looked, how our surroundings looked, were evidently more important to this man I had chosen to live with than how I was feeling.

This was not the first but the second effort I made to eradicate life's woes by ingesting Valium, then the drug of choice for anxiety and presumably for depression, even though depression was one of the results of taking this drug. I had been taking the Valium that was prescribed by my gynecologist, after I relayed to him some of the heaviness of my life when I was living with my mentally deranged husband at the country store. As he handed me a prescription for Valium, the doctor, whom I now recognize I allowed to be yet another authority figure, a power-wielding patriarch, in my life, advised that I go home and bake cookies with my girls. His advice came at the time when eighteen, yes, *eighteen* loaves of bread plus pies and, yes, cookies were paraded daily downstairs from our apartment over the store to the counter by the cash register. With this piece of paper the doctor opened a door to immediate but short-lived relief from pressure. The relief was always palpable. But I did not know that if depression was an enemy, Valium over time inspired that enemy to even greater downdrafts.

The first effort to do myself in took place in 1978. I had just returned from Oregon, where an emotional massacre took place over the week that I and two of my three brothers sorted and packed the contents of our parents' home. Our mother had died just months before, and our father was living with one of my brothers. On this late winter day I left my office at the ski resort and sat hidden in a snowbank as I swallowed a handful of Valium. Then I walked myself into the administration office and told someone what I had just done. I don't recall the trip to Rutland; I do remember receiving a box of candy from a ski writer from Boston who had expected to find me on duty at the mountain and not in the psychiatric ward of the Rutland Regional Medical Center. I stayed only long enough to learn from the administering physician, a white-haired patriarch who, in my myopic fog, seemed to have stepped out of an Old Master painting, that if I didn't rally round, my children would be put into foster care. I left in such a hurry that I don't think I even checked out. After what was probably less than a 24-hour interval of enforced bed rest, not even motherhood could cajole me from the Valium-induced despair that tracked me. But what nobody but me knows is that when I escaped to the hospital parking lot, where my car was thoughtfully waiting, I didn't go straight home to East Poultney. Instead I made the hour-plus drive to Montpelier. And why? Because that's where Joe lived (this was before we moved in together). He had not been in touch with me while I was in the hospital and he was not home when I arrived at his door. The road back to East Poultney that night was long indeed.

My effort to escape reality by ingesting too much Valium went unnoticed by anyone until the second attempt some years later. As the weight of my husband's illness drilled ever deeper into our family life and marriage, and before he left us, I had discovered that relief came only minutes after taking a pill, relief that allowed me to ignore the fact that with each pill I was becoming increasingly depressed. Valium is a depressant and the pill itself, and the relief, are addictive. This addiction continued even after my husband moved out of state. I could always get refills without reconnecting with my doctor. The drugstore was just down the street in Poultney.

Doubtless Valium was a key player one night before Christmas when I was trying to rally my young daughters for a cookie-making session. But while Valium had a stranglehold on me, a Christmas episode of *The Andy Griffith Show* had my girls captivated. I invited them to come help me in the kitchen. They didn't leave the television. I started screaming, rushed into the living room, tore the plug of the small portable television set out of the wall, took this competitor to the door (we lived above the store) and threw it two stories down onto the ground. The girls rushed to a neighbor's house crying, "Something is wrong with our Mommy." And how right they were! Sipping wine while nibbling on cookie dough — plus Valium — let's face it, is like lighting a match over the open nozzle of a gasoline can. In fact, together they created the perfect storm.

Adding fuel to fire in the second attempt I made to disappear was a relationship that defied my logic. Joe and I lived together, but why weren't we married? I think I may have asked this question once. His veiled allusions to "things aren't always as they seem" did nothing to assuage my anxiety. Only years later did I realize that he may have been keeping another family, a small unit of woman and one daughter. Secrets don't sit well with intimacy; Valium bodes ill in the system; I ended up having my stomach pumped. The druggist in Poultney, where I used to live, who had obliged me over the years with refills on my prescription, cut me off. I thought about life — or not living — on a summer night in the field outside the Montpelier house. I held a razor blade. The crickets were in fine tune. There was a moon. Everything seemed such a waste that I didn't even scratch myself.

Years before, I was the wife in James Thurber's one-act play *The Unicorn in the Garden*, a plot that turns the tables from the mentally ill person into the supposed sane, and vice versa.

This had happened to me.

The years of trying to hold things together and supporting my family and without childcare assistance had taken their toll. I was never going to get better remaining in this relationship with Joe that had begun to suffocate me. Weekends I would leave the house we shared, walking sometimes six or ten miles on roads around our property. I couldn't breathe in this house of secrets, in a relationship where nothing I did ever seemed to be enough. On the day I vacated the property, headed for my new position as marketing director at a New Hampshire resort, my VW Beetle was laden with personal effects and potted plants. Until the house sold, my younger daughter would remain here to keep watch. Joe brought sandwiches for a lunch that we ate outside in the sun before I drove the Volkswagen away. This no-longer-live-in companion's parting words to me were: "You tried too hard."

Sweetness and light … nothing was right. Not a complete patsy, I got in a few parting salvos of my own. On the day he announced he was going on a holiday with another woman (while we were still living together), I baked a blueberry pie. Now, Joe loved my blueberry pie. I left one, baked and luscious, sitting on his car hood before he left for the weekend. How and where did he enjoy it? Who knows? But he was not one to waste opportunity. When he came home he declared, "She's not like you." His next move, minutes later, was to take me down to the basement, away from anyone who might have been upstairs, and make quite frenetic love to me. Perhaps his weekend had not gone so well. He was conflicted. I was moving into emotional survival mode.

And don't let me forget the tractor. Our property was expansive and required, in addition to the manicuring of a yard, the occasional mowing of a field graced by a stone wall. To accomplish this Joe used a tractor mower. When he had officially left our love nest, the tractor stayed behind. I knew how to use it. He had advised that it might be low on oil. So sad. It was. I burned out the motor one Saturday morning. This sent me in a frenzy to a hardware store to pick up a rental mower. That mower failed to perform and so I picked up another. Some women, when they find themselves in these situations, have a succession of lovers. I just had a succession of lawn mowers, as well as many hours spent over one weekend, tissues in hand, on the living room couch listening over and over and over again to a recording of tenors singing the most poignant arias of Italian opera, on a turntable that Joe had gifted to me.

During this time, unbeknownst to me, Joe, whose handle on the CB radio was Silver Fox, purchased a condominium on the other side of town. He announced he was moving out of our house. I helped him pack, and that's when I started running. Every evening I would go to the Montpelier High School track. The first night I only ran around once, amounting to about one quarter of a mile. I praised myself lavishly and returned the next night for a half mile and every evening added distance to my workout. Eventually I was doing five miles a day, a habit — perhaps another addiction — that moved successfully with me to New Hampshire and back to Manhattan.

I even ran through the streets of Tbilisi, in Georgia, which was still part of the former Soviet Union, when I visited in 1986. How did I get there? I was the high bidder at an auction sponsored by Physicians for Social Responsibility and Project Harmony. For $1,200 I became part of a group of New Englanders escorted by a husband-and-wife team who were directors of the World Center Fellowship in New Hampshire's White Mountains. Born in East Germany during World War II to an antifascist family, Christoph Schmauch has made international relations, especially east–west relations, and world peace his life's work. Kathryn Schmauch is an activist in women's issues worldwide.

Our group's mission was to meet with peace groups in assorted cities. In Tbilisi we sat in a café at small tables for two. My companion for the hour or so we were there was a professor of linguistics. His suavity and charisma would have suited him well on Madison Avenue. The conversation was a bit one-sided, by choice. There were so few minutes in which to share information that rolled off my tongue about issues and products he didn't know about. In linguistics, for example, had he read the newly published book *Gödel, Escher, Bach*? No, he had not, even though this book had been out for months. Upon returning to Montpelier I mailed him a copy that I hope he received.

As immersive as the cross-cultural world was, so was the introduction to my travel mates from Montpelier, all older than I, and of the ilk who staged demonstrations outside the statehouse. I was disdainful then of people who had the time to protest (although I would join them today) about issues that always appeared to be left-leaning while I was trying to fit the mold of the socially progressive, financially conservative stereotype that Joe preferred me to be. He meanwhile espoused Republican values, including the idea that "for the public good" workers needed to be sacrificed in coal mines. At the time I didn't realize that this was a world view so far removed from mine that this alone would be enough to cause a relationship rift. While in the Soviet Union, the New Englanders around me continued to surprise me by showing that they were ardent supporters of our country and not the flag burners I thought they might be.

Alla, our guide, was a woman of my age who had survived the German invasion of St. Petersburg in June 1941, during World War II. Her father's name is among the heroes listed on the war memorial in Leningrad that commemorates the city's nine-hundred-day siege against the Nazis. Alla and her mother were sent to the country during the siege, but she recalls returning to where she once lived. Left was a surreal impression, like something from a Salvador Dali painting, of walls knocked out of the flat but a piano still intact. Books and furniture had been burned for heat. Citizens were ordered out into the street when spring came, to pick up corpses and prevent the outbreak of disease.

To her I gifted my paperback copy of *A Distant Mirror,* which had passed the scrutiny of officials checking our reading material as we went through customs at the airport. (I didn't get around to reading this marvel until decades later.) Alla's itinerary was extensive, shuttling us from Moscow to St. Petersburg and on to Tbilisi, then to Yerevan in Armenia and to Baku in Azerbaijan. Tbilisi was a highlight, reminiscent of a favorite Italian destination, even though it had been sacked and plundered countless times. At the opera one night the audience around me was as interesting as the improvised *The Love for Three Oranges* on the stage. Even in these lean times, the women were elegantly dressed, having called on their local seamstresses to create the dresses that were crowned by black coifs. In our hotel dining room, open only to hotel guests, the apples were shriveled. The wait staff could have been in service on a luxury cruise ship.

En route by bus from Tbilisi to Yerevan, Armenia, we encountered a roadblock half-way into our journey. We were deterred from going through a mountain pass where the night before a dozen people had died when their bus slipped off the road. The pass was closed, although now, twenty-four hours later, no word of either the accident or the closing of a major highway had reached tourism authorities, even as this country was exploring space. Our bus driver rescued us from hunger by purchasing a large loaf of warm bread. This, along with liverwurst, carrots and apples, was our make-do, in-transit lunch as we returned to Tbilisi to board an overnight train for Yerevan. My purse strap was wrapped tightly around my wrist as I hugged my pillow on the top bunk of a four-bunk compartment. The other three bunks were occupied by Soviet men to whom I had never been introduced. After the commotion of a rock hurled at a window three sleeping cars from mine, the next morning a hostess served tea and an orange. I stood in the corridor removing myself from the reality of my roommates and flying rocks, becoming for a few minute the only heroine I could conjure up — Anna Karenina.

We then flew from Yerevan to Baku, the capital of Azerbaijan. Seated next to me while on this flight was a lawyer from Hamburg in West Germany. He was leading a group of technicians on a first-time tour of the Soviet Union.

What were his impressions, I asked?

"Very disappointing," he said, "to find the primitive conditions after hearing how good things are when I listen to radio out of East Germany."

"And yours?" he asked.

"I can't believe," I said, "that this is the country that created Sputnik, that is our arch rival in the arms race and even now is pioneering space research, even while little old women in black are sweeping major city streets with handmade brooms."

And I mentioned other things I had seen which left an impression: in Leningrad, a man with a small ice pick chipping away at the ice on a roadside curb; in Tbilisi, four men on their haunches huddled around the carcass of a sheep in a courtyard, only a few blocks from the hub of Georgia's capital; in an Intourist hotel, a public restroom offering a hole in the floor for a toilet.

I told him about the carpet-making factory in an Armenian village where girls ages fifteen to twenty-five performed the functions of machines, hands flying faster than the eye could follow, pulling, knotting and cutting yarns to create hand-made Oriental rugs. Pale and stoop-shouldered, they were not allowed to weave after age twenty-five because the work is hard on the eyes.

But mostly I told him about the old women, the two who emerged from a darkened corridor lugging a tub of wash water between them to be dumped into the street, those countless old women in black out in the streets, sweeping, sweeping, sweeping with brooms hand-made of clumps of brush that look like heather.

Communications in Georgia were at best scanty and this was way before cell phones. Yet Leonid Brezhnev et al. were doubtless imbibing shots of vodka as the Russian space program was, for the time being, on its way to overtaking ours.

Straws can break the backs of both camels and people. Not long after this adventure I resigned from the newspaper to take a position as marketing director for a condominium resort being developed on a mountainside in central Vermont. The presiding Governor of Vermont, Madeleine Kunin, and I often squared off on early-evening television shows when we were interviewed as to the progress — and desirability — of this project. I had to be pro-project; Governor Kunin was not. True confession: Even I knew that five hundred units were too many, and my heart wasn't in this promotion.

The owner of a New Hampshire ski resort asked me to be his marketing director. My forwarded mail from my previous residence included a Jewish periodical that I received while working on the *Times-Argus*. The post office in my new community was tiny, and whose mail came from where was doubtless broadcast by the postmistress. For the duration I worked for him, my boss believed I was Jewish and even apologized to me when he made an anti-Semitic joke. I didn't bother to persuade him otherwise.

Truth over People

I ask myself, "Do I value Truth over People?'
and I answer "Yes"
for without Truth there is no value
and People slip through the cracks
of Lies until lives lie extinguished
in the detritus of "Mis-truths."
I prefer not to sort through these ashes,
rather to see Truth through People
for whom Phoenixes are fantasies
shelved to make room for simple Facts.

Christmas New Hampshire 1987

Dear All,
Some mornings when I wake up in New Hampshire's White Mountains I wonder: *Just why am I here?* Are there reasons I've plunked myself in such beautiful surroundings on the one hand and isolation on the other? What are the paths from here?

The reasons might include a nearly five-mile jogging route at my doorstep and an Olympic-size swimming pool for *après* run, no noise, no hassle getting to and from work, clean air.

This has been a year to pull body and mind together ... to regain a sense of "self" that had been substantially jostled for the past several years. And, most important, it has been a time to get to know my two wonderful daughters, now young women, in a tranquil setting. Both are living with me for the time being.

It has been a year of hard and fulfilling work, and a year offering the most incredible journey I've ever taken.

In mid fall (October 19, 1987, Black Monday) I flew from JFK Airport to India with a small tour group put together by a university alumni department. From first setting foot in New Delhi, and for the subsequent three weeks of adventure that unfolded, I was led through the northeastern state of Rajasthan, which means "lands of kings" and where we were royally wined and dined in palaces with marble halls; to Agra and the Taj Mahal; to the river Ganga in Varanasi, where literally hundreds of people at sunrise bathe and worship in the water; and to Kathmandu, Nepal, for several days surrounded by the spectacular Himalayas.

I've pondered how to describe my experiences. Passages from several pertinent books help mightily:

From *Freedom at Midnight*, by Larry Collins and Dominique Lapierre:

From a thousand, tens of thousands of mud-brick huts speckling the great Punjab plain it came, the smoke of India's meal-time fires.

123

And from Peter Matthiessen's *The Snow Leopard*:

Confronted with the pain of Asia, one cannot look and cannot turn away.

Saris, Birds and Butterflies

From Delhi Belly to Kathmandu,
our guide, we owe it all to you.
We're now well-versed in lots of lore
from Sherpa to Shiva, Akbar to Babur.
We've bitten dust and fondled silk,
from curds to custards drunk your milk,
witnessed Diwali, slept like kings,
bounced on elephants, soared with wings.
Jasmine and jasper, black-horned fawns
made their points amid the throngs.
Thatch and wood, dung and brick,
wheat and millet, rice to pick ...
saris, birds and butterflies
singing through the parched-earth eyes ...
roads where "mightier than thou" applies
to bike and goat and cow ...
beggar fingers, stubs of joints,
children, babies, cast their marks.
From Hindu to Muslim, Sikh to Parsi
we've met a complex humanity.
Forget the adage that worlds get smalle.
Our potentials expand as the mountains get taller.
You gave us a gift we can never repay.
Thank you, our guide, for each wonderful day.

On the Road Again

When the appealing, four-color solicitation inviting me to India first arrived in my New Hampshire post box, I was immediately hooked. Quite frankly, the sunshine-filled photos compelled me to book this journey, despite the fact that it would require three weeks (instead of the allotted two vacation weeks) away from my desk. I justified to myself that I had worked seven days a week for well over a year — and didn't I deserve that extra week, after all?

Seemingly I did not. Nor, as it turned out, did I deserve to remain in this tiny valley in a condominium I had purchased from the resort owner, piecing together an existence, even as my youngest daughter laughed her head off inside the condo one night watching me run from my car to the door, away from the visiting black bear. Sometimes on my daily run around the backroads of the resort I encountered wildlife. The mother moose and her baby followed me down the road. I positioned myself so as to be one with the next tree and watched them pass, scarcely daring to breathe, only moving my eyes to follow their saunter. In late summer I heard what I thought were children laughing down a lane that connected with this road. I looked. The voices were not of humans but of black bears working away at the blackberries. Not stopping to count, but assuming there was a mother with cubs, I focused on what I could remember about bear habits. First, they have difficulty running downhill. Not waiting for a second fact, in seconds I was running as fast as I could away from them.

Little did I know that my journey to India would provoke yet another change. The previous winter I had helped accomplish the highest number of skier days this New Hampshire resort had ever known. The fact that it had been a snow-filled winter played a part in this achievement, as did (I hoped) some of my marketing strategies. But I never received a pat on the back from anyone.

I did receive attention, however, when I completed the annual project of producing a newly designed (by me) brochure that led one friend of the resort owner to ask: "What are you trying to do? Win an award for your collateral?" The brochure was beautiful, leaving behind the "everything but the kitchen sink" approach that had been the resort's norm.

Shortly after the brochure was ready to send out and my marketing team was armed with distribution instructions, I went to India. Evidently in retrospect I didn't "deserve" to take this journey and I broke the vacation days rule to do so. As time goes by, I understand that the word "deserve" has no place in the litany of expectations and that perhaps the only people who truly "deserve" are those who can count on where their next meal is coming from because they've already achieved an elevated status.

India helped put all of this in perspective. I flew for hours on Air India to arrive at dawn. Outside the New Delhi airport, the theater of street life is less about pathos and more about getting a good night's sleep on whatever cart hooked to a patient ox may be available. I had flown away from the economic disaster that came to be known as the Black Monday stock market crash. I first heard of this slide into the economic abyss just before boarding my plane at JFK Airport. I had chosen to fly Air India in order to begin immersing myself immediately in a new culture. The colorful costumes of fellow passengers and the smells of native food delivered by sari-clad hostesses stimulated my senses. Three weeks later, the poverty I saw seared my brain and filled it with words like dignity, courage and, yes, even joy. People can live with little to nothing. Whatever the Black Monday stock crash left behind for me would be simply a place from which I would begin again.

The bus waited for our group outside the carpet store in New Delhi where I succumbed to a condition that I liken to a fever and that resulted in my buying three Oriental rugs that were small enough to wedge into my suitcase. Back on the bus I saw a beggar gesturing to me through the closed window. Leprosy ravaged the arms of this beggar, a mother, holding the thin bundle that was her baby.

This tortured scene became one of my starting places, as was the shock I felt when, over lunch in a palace rife with the lore of the Raj, a man serving out table asked: "What would Memsahib like to drink?" I was Memsahib. This appellation felt as comfortable as a well-worn slipper, as did the visages of peacocks preening in the courtyard.

A man I met over drinks at the Taj Mahal, an elegant hotel in New Delhi, invited me to a soccer match. To accept meant I would miss the group foray to the often-filmed site India Gate, where Lord Mountbatten stood at attention during the raising of the Indian national flag. My new acquaintance held more interest for me at the time. The game was held in the Jawaharlal Nehru Stadium, which seats 60,000. The packed masses were cordoned off in sections for the sake of crowd control, as winners and losers were known to incite game-induced riots. The air was charged as we went through the security gates. We were requested not to enter with water bottles or cameras, as these could become instruments of war in the event of a riot. On the benches sat slight, skinny-legged men.

During one van ride through New Delhi we saw men on their hands and knees using grass clippers to cut by hand a very large lawn. A man in our group asked: "Why are they cutting the grass with those hand clippers? Why don't they use lawn mowers?" I hope he eventually answered his own question.

Meanwhile, I had my own questions to answer. Why did a bevy of sari-clad young women, bright as butterflies, tie a tea cup to a slender rope to lower into the well they had walked far in the heat from their village to reach? Why did a hut made of dung have no furnishings but only a much-scoured, cast-iron skillet? Why were the young farmer's children untreated for sores that all but oozed on our table as we shared a farm-to-table lunch years before this concept became trendy? And why, when people had already walked on the moon, were shopkeepers here computing with an abacus?

Some months after returning from India, once again a moving van was at my door. I was bound — again — for Manhattan. My work in New Hampshire's White Mountains had been terminated.

Although I didn't know this, other people did: My playing fields at two Vermont ski resorts and now at one in New Hampshire had shrunk, while I had grown professionally. The Indian sampler seduced me in ways that soon begin to nag. Interesting people? Sunshine? Stimulation? I had been allowing myself to become spiritually and culturally destitute.

One of my several forays from New Hampshire to New York as I searched for a way out of the mountains of New England found me standing in front a bank of pay phones in Grand Central Station. Thick phone books dangling from chains promised entrée to a world where I needed to be. They harbored promises of a career in writing advertising copy, perhaps. Because work until now had just fallen into my lap, I knew nothing about how to apply for a job. Any zeal I had mustered for these cold calls dwindled faster than my supply of dimes did.

On yet another effort to scale the ramparts to a professional career in New York, I drove from New Hampshire to Manhattan to interview with some of the country's leading travel-related public relations firms. On one unsuccessful foray, I learned a life lesson. Be sure to eat before you go on interviews. I didn't. By mid-afternoon, during what would be the last conversation of this kind I ever hoped to have, I suddenly saw myself, nearly fifty years old, in the position of supplicant, and my anxiety and frustration surfaced as tears in front of the woman who was interviewing me. She and her husband owned the company. She was kind. In fact, she later hired one of my daughters to work with her team. But there was no job offering for me. I went back to my Volkswagen, parked on a Manhattan street. As I opened the Beetle's door to get in, a taxi came swooping by, ripping the door nearly off its hinges. Misty-eyed, I drove the over three-hundred miles back to New Hampshire, clutching with one hand the door and with the other the steering wheel. I was totally rudderless.

Before I could leave New England, I needed to sell my condominium for cash. Eventually a sale went through. In the meantime I patched together an income from a few marketing projects here and there, even hiring a man I'll call C. to help with my work. Engaging and well spoken, C. convinced me that investing in a business his friend in Florida was starting was a no-brainer. When he told me later about the sapphire ring he had bought his girlfriend, I realized what I had done for him. That was $10,000 of sheer stupidity — mine to own. We were working together on a public relations project that had come my way. The project required printing and folding press releases and stuffing them into envelopes addressed to regional media. He took the stuffing project home with him to Vermont and disappeared. Unbeknownst to me at the time, because of this colleague's deviousness, the client was not properly serviced. The paperwork is long gone and I don't even remember the product we were promoting. If I could track down those long-ago entrepreneurs, I would refund their retainer.

Making good decisions doesn't always come naturally. After India and Nepal I was eager to become a butterfly again. Nepal had made such an impression on me that I applied to teach English with the Peace Corps and was accepted for a position in Nepal. Only when I woke up did I realize that with one still-dependent daughter, traveling long distances for extended periods of time must be curtailed. I withdrew my application.

Dust and Motes

We've cleaned out many houses, you and I,
sturdily trudging the deep furrows of detritus,
sorting, sifting through dust and motes of those must go,
selecting only memories hard-pressed, mad to forsake.

Easter New Hampshire 1988

Perhaps there won't be a fireplace in the next place I live. But the props will all be there: the Vasarely poster gifted to a husband on an anniversary and that later went unclaimed; the russet and green oil painting depicting the Tuscan hills where happy days marked the beginning — and end — of our married love; the gold-framed, handwoven cloth from Rajasthan, cloth now trapped under glass to imprison the smell of Indian dung and dust; the matched Pompeii-style water jugs, Italian antiques from a grandfather I never knew; a cloisonné lamp; china showpieces; assorted Oriental and Chinese rugs; tapestries from the workshop of Gobelin; boxes of books.

These will, with more or less grace, follow me to my next domain, leaving behind another shell, a dead fire to be relit by new and optimistic actors.

This collection of clutter that costs, variously, several hundred or several thousand dollars to move, depending on whether the truck is U-Haul or Mayflower, I've come to depend on as the only significantly stable furnishings of my life.

The marriage came and went. The passionate affair ended. The babies grew. The children were nearly launched. The jobs, a litany of failures and successes, chiseled away at time.

Yet another move is pending. Doesn't serve any purpose to recount how many tons of paper, stacks of cardboard boxes and aching backs there have been before reaching this point. The point isn't significant, no more the motion and the change.

Moving, though, always creates dilemmas. What to do, for instance, with the artifacts triumphantly removed from a past lover's wall and flung in fury in an empty drawer? "Indian giver," he cried. "Not for another woman's eyes," I replied.

What about the books, collected but not culled these many years, that reflect a peculiar taste for people and poets: biographies that in their reading created curious friends; poetry that sparked my own unpublished verse?

And silly things, like spices: the jar of whole nutmeg that's probably traveled six times and still isn't used up; the sage and ginger salvaged from my mother's home when her house was packed for the last time some years ago.

We're not, some would have us believe, our things. But they are partly our stage, that which surrounds us on a rainy day before the fire, sitting reading, alone, with the mountains shrouded in mist and Easter passing by. There are resurrections in spring of all kinds of hope. Perhaps the constancy of this theater is what these things are all about — a bit of hope.

Savory and Sweet

Spices savory and sweet
stored in cupboards high above the counter,
although accessible to Mother,
require climbing on a stool
to peer past them to yellowed boxes marked by X,
poison and danger alongside alum
pulled out for canker sores
responding well to the puckering foment inside her mouth,
tasted again when the Japanese quince blossoms became hard,
tart fruit best laid aside for jelly.

Guardian Angels

At this juncture I came to understand that some people in our lives serve, alive or dead, as guardian angels. One appeared in the form of a ski writer who wrote for *Vogue*, among other publications. Her cheeky commentary included thoughts about vestal virgins being flung from a Vermont mountain. She may have had me in mind. I had come to know her through my corporate duties as head of public relations at several New England ski resorts. She kindly introduced me to a well-regarded public relations consultancy in New York City. There I met the successful entrepreneur who would be my new boss — the boss who, within a few weeks of hiring me, sent me off to her preferred hairdresser, who was asked to style the country and mountains out of the girl.

All was going well, I thought. My boss and I were alone in a taxi when she shared with me her annoyance that her household staff didn't do what she asked. I clucked sympathetically. In retrospect this was a veiled threat, as later she warned me that I wasn't to waste time on her watch writing thank-you notes to the journalists who had kindly paid attention to her clients in newspapers and magazines. In the end I was just one in the lineup of carnival ducks she took out on a whim. Doesn't matter now. Did then. Once again I was without remuneration, with another condo, recently purchased (this one on the north shore of Staten Island), to pay for. I landed in the unemployment office until I was able to piece together my own clientele, some kind of miracle that even now defies logic when I try to explain how I did it.

This dismissal gave me a pause — and a long one — to think about what was becoming my growing portfolio, a litany of failures on the professional front, all directly related to my approach to my work. I suspect I left little to no room for my supervisors. Because it's my nature to throw myself wholeheartedly into any project at my fingertips, my energy was, I am certain now, overbearing. The results of my work spoke for themselves, achieving positive effects on bottom lines on spread sheets I was never introduced to. However, looking back, order and decorum when I was around were doubtless challenged. Quite simply, I set my own priorities and practiced my own style. I was not easy to manage.

Decades have disappeared since those long days when I amused my unemployed self by taking on the aesthetics of Richmond Boulevard between the Staten Island Ferry Terminal and my Staten Island condominium. Armed with plastic gloves and big plastic garbage bags, I tackled the displays that disenfranchised souls leave behind. Tumbled about the weeds around the bases of trees lining the boulevard was one empty whisky or wine bottle after another. The clean-up pace was slow and hot and dirty. People stopped and asked me: "Why are you doing this?" "Because I can," I replied, "and so can you." Making a difference when there was nothing else to do salved the hurt imposed by empty and lonely days. One day became much brighter when a paper bag that was submerged in the weeds fell apart in my hands, revealing dollar bills of various denominations. I was holding a cache that would not make me rich, but it was enough to signify that luck was on my side. Or at least that was the value I attached to the discovery, stuffing the bills in the pockets of my shorts.

The clean-up continued, as did the summer. A client from the agency where I no longer worked contacted me. He would like to leave the agency and hire me. This was a beginning. I knew of a woman from California whose public relations reputation was stellar. I reached out to her and asked if she might like some assistance out of New York on behalf of her five-star clients. In ensuing weeks, yes, she would.

Professionally I was ready to be in full gear. A colleague contacted me. I had worked with her at the office where I wrote thank you notes to journalists that got me fired. She lived uptown, at 86th Street and Madison Avenue. She suggested that in exchange for a monthly stipend I might use her apartment as my business base. She also had been terminated and was in a start-up mode. We could help each other. Like a milkman making my rounds, I began my day at Sea Containers' offices on 46th Street, not far from Grand Central Station. Here I worked for my newfound California mentor on behalf of her client, Orient-Express Hotels, Trains & Cruises, a division of the London-headquartered Sea

Containers. (This company later rebranded as Belmond: Luxury Hotels, River Cruises, Trains and Safaris. In December 2018 it was sold for $2.8 billion to LVMH Moët Hennessy Louis Vuitton, a Paris-based company that went on to purchase Cartier.)

I had a desk and telephone in a corporate setting that was civil and serene, thanks in great part to the managing director and his lovely assistant, Marie-Therese Afif. She to this day is a very dear friend. My day continued uptown with a handful of staff who quickly began to outgrow the Upper East Side apartment.

Stepping into the limelight, Sara Widness Communications was in an enviable position thanks to the prestige that came with representing Orient-Express Hotels, Trains & Cruises. Building a client roster was, quite simply, fun. So was collaborating with my friend Maggie Kerrigan, who had recently left her post with the New Zealand Tourism Board in Santa Monica, California. She was living with me on Staten Island. Plans were afoot to join forces professionally. We wrote a business plan that (like the phrase from the movie *Field of Dreams*, "If you build it they will come") presaged what would become a successful enterprise in just a few years. Sadly, her father was dying and her mother became ill. Maggie left New York to return to New Zealand, never to live in the United States again.

Without Maggie, the growing pains at Sara Widness Communications intensified. The connection with my California mentor paid generously. This affiliation also led to an invitation from the tourism powers-that-be of Rio de Janeiro to work on that city's behalf. Because this contract would not have come to me were it not for the connection with the savvy California businesswoman, I paid her $1,000 of the Rio contract every month. She would never have expected this, but I was returning in the only way I could the great good luck that her trust in me had brought me. I felt that doing this was an unwritten obligation to honor the wisdom that one good turn deserves another. I'm not even sure that she understood why I needed to do this.

The world I entered on behalf of her clients and their interests was grand, peopled by multi-linguists wearing haute couture who sometimes spoke with those plummy accents you hear on National Public Radio, accents that come from adapting an American upbringing to international shores and vice versa. In this universe of privilege, a bucket of long-stemmed roses was doubtless *de rigueur,* but for me it became a source of enchantment. Once I surpassed sixteen as I counted the number of stems shorn of thorns just over there on the Grand Canal of Venice at Hotel Cipriani. Or as Rimbaud, wrote: "… the sky and sea entice to the marble stairway whole mobs of brash young roses."

Truth Must Have Its Way

Between heart and silence lies truth.
The heart speaks.
But can we hear?
Or does commitment's cacophony
swallow "I love yous"
until the heart can bear
no longer to sustain the voice?
Between heart and silence lies truth.
Silence speaks
But can we hear?
Or do risks' possibilities
subsume "I love yous"
until silence is clear
that truth must have its way with us.

Bucking the Tides

I undertook three times the task of bucking the tide of public sentiment in those years I was conducting public relations projects from my New York office. Once was when I brought journalists to a South Africa that was still in the throes of apartheid. Another was when I escorted journalists to Myanmar (Burma) when the United States was to have nothing to do with that country. And the third was when I invited journalists to Rio de Janeiro at a time when most publications were fearful of sending their staff there because of perceived physical danger. I could feel the alienation of the young people we met in Cape Town. They weren't hostile but they did have attitude and perhaps chips on their shoulders. After all, their country was being shamed by ours. The Burmese were just genuinely happy to see us, even those Burmese citizens who, I suspect, were filling dual roles, acting as guides on behalf of the military. Rio was a different matter. The city was turning in on itself, not understanding (at least on the surface) why people would not want to come to such a beautiful destination. I think the city was experiencing a collective paranoia in reaction to highly publicized shootings and crimes.

When carrying out public relations duties, charm and discretion were called upon at all times. Charm, however, could be tested. I was escorting a group of American travel journalists to Myanmar, which at the time was still under a bell jar of politically imposed sanctions. The writers were warned in advance that they should not disclose their profession as journalists to authorities in Myanmar, where American journalists were unwelcome. Basically we were not even supposed to be there. Upon arrival at the airport in Yangon (Rangoon), the travel editor of a major daily newspaper broke ranks. Her disclosure to the authorities evoked long minutes of anxiety. These officials were relentlessly harsh. We were held hostage at the airport until the guide assigned to us sorted things out.

In Rio de Janeiro I was hosting a band of journalists. Because of the size of this group, we were all assigned to stay at different hotels. One writer complained that she was not lodged at what she perceived to be the best hotel. I took her aside and suggested that as she seemed not to be enjoying this trip, perhaps I could get her flown out on the first plane the next morning. She subsided. Another twosome, ardent vegetarians, advised me during every meal in Rio that they couldn't eat this or that, and they asked how could I help. Remember that this is the home of *churrasqueria*. Somewhere I have a photo of myself smiling wanly across the table at them over the last lunch, before which I had managed to contract a bout of dyspepsia. Nerves, perhaps?

Nerves surfaced often in these days. Looking back, I understand that in life and in business I have been a risk taker. Let's look at business. In those days clients rarely came to our company with a clear idea of what we might achieve for them, other than getting them ink in *Travel & Leisure* and a handful of other upscale travel publications. Oh, yes, exposure on national television would be great, too. Even though in elementary and high school I was always the klutz when playing competitive sports (in fact, I was never invited onto teams), I was now on a playing field with countless opportunities for goals that I delighted in.

Red flag. Hubris lurks around this intersection. Sometimes I would create opportunities for clients based on what I thought was good for them and not necessarily based on what they wanted. Sometimes these opportunities had nothing to do with media coverage but explored the arenas of charitable donations. On behalf of Orient-Express Hotels, Trains & Cruises I would secure — with the client's permission — their donations of a gift to travel, for example, on the Venice Simplon-Orient-Express, the fabled train. These trips were usually gifted to auctions from which charitable organizations could raise money. My client in turn would receive top billing in the collateral used to promote some kind of grand event. Nine times out of ten this was a "win-win" scenario for all concerned, including our agency. And these donations helped me to feel, rightly or wrongly, that I was helping to create something of value to mankind.

But once the donation backfired. The winner of an auction prize, a trip for two on the Venice Simplon-Orient-Express, marched into my office one day demanding I pay him the money he had spent at the auction to secure the trip. He alleged some legal issue (there was none) with the terms of the donation. He threatened to go to my client if I didn't pay him something between $4,000 and $5,000. The last thing an agency wants is any kind of hassle with a client. So I paid this man his "blood money" and erased this extortion from my mind. Only now do I understand that this was a scam that allowed the man to look good before the organization hosting the auction. He had created a tax deduction, perhaps even took the train journey, and then he got all his money back by pushing my arm up my back. Who knows? Shortly after this, someone with his last name was exposed in local newspapers for fraud and was sent to cool his heels in jail. Perhaps he already knew his own cash flow was going to be strapped. I never took the time to connect the dots precisely.

Toward the end of my company's tenure with the London office, another dragon reared his head. Regularly, we sent writers on a complimentary basis to the hotels, trains and cruises we represented. The gentleman's agreement was that journalists would file stories about their experiences. Some clients hosted a writer's travel companion at no cost; others asked for a companion fee. One writer was annoyed when he requested from our office complimentary travel for his wife to travel with him on the Venice Simplon-Orient-Express. We denied him because of the client-dictated protocol that limited the number of traveling companions who could be accommodated. He then went directly to the London office and lodged a complaint against me. He rocked the boat. At the same time and unbeknownst to me, another writer had been trying to get through to me on the phone to communicate her desire to travel on the Venice Simplon-Orient-Express. This was the summer of 2002, only months after 9/11 and the pending collapse of my company. Her messages never reached me. The writer got fed up and lodged her complaint with the client in London.

I was traveling in China when a fax from the corporate office in London caught up with me. The wonderful woman in London for whom I'd had the pleasure of working for several years had been replaced. As often happens when a new manager is brought in, the new manager wanted to bring in his or her own team. Brandishing the aforementioned prompts hinting at dereliction of my duties, London severed their contract with our company via a fax I received on a machine in the administration office of a Chinese boarding school where I was on a brief, volunteer assignment teaching English. I tried not to think about how and even if

I could rebuild my public relations consultancy.

My former London manager had over the years assembled a remarkable team of communication mavens all over the world. They were gracious, articulate and kind. And I think we all respected each other and the work we did for this prestigious company. This was team sports at its finest, with enough room on the playing field for everyone to score their own goals. We were an appreciative audience for one another.

Difficulties aside, the sheer fun of dressing to the nines and sipping in solitude a glass of champagne before meeting my writer guests and hosts for dinner in the candle- and chandelier-lit dining room at one of their elegant hotels always amused me. As the clock ticked, I could be whoever I wanted to be in a world as resplendent and as hermetically sealed as a Fabergé egg.

Sherry

Afternoons I grab some ice
on which I pour the sherry,
a habit leading into nights
less lonely — and quite merry.

Disappearing Decades

In the early 1990s I was in my early fifties and playing on a very big stage as a female WASP (White Anglo-Saxon Protestant) with no capital and no sugar daddy or financial backer — except for credit cards. My bit part as I waded into the lifestyle of a sybarite included embarking on a daily sea voyage on the Staten Island Ferry across New York Harbor, challenging the skyline with "OK, Manhattan, what do you have for me today?" Plenty, so it seemed, and more and more as time went on. A decade later, this boutique public relations enterprise had outgrown its Upper East Side home; staff were bumping into each other trying to get at the too-few computers. The young woman who was now my business partner, a woman the same age as my eldest daughter, insisted we needed a larger office. We located a loft space in the Leica Building on Broadway and Bond.

A Vermont friend helped to refurbish this sunny space. My credit card made possible the purchase of IKEA furniture. Visitors to the office sometimes expressed that they could live in this lovely environment. Actually this happened for a few weeks, when a writer I had hosted at lunch at the 21 Club said her apartment was being repainted and asked if she could use a desk in our office at night, when she had to make business calls to China. After several weeks her suitcases were discovered in the storage cabinets. She was asked to leave.

I observed my colleagues, other public relations mavens and journalists, living the privileged life of wining and dining in Manhattan on behalf of clients. Perhaps some considered as their birthright dining on risotto tucked under a mantle of real gold leaf. My reaction was always like that of Dorothy when she was suddenly out of Kansas — complete awe at the affluence and arrogance of the likes of Donald Trump. His table of choice was positioned practically in the foyer of 21 Club. Anyone approaching the banquettes nearly tripped over him. In the 1990s he was creating his own theatrical strategies.

As business grew, our office staff expanded. I am sad when I recall that at the request of a mutual colleague I arranged to meet a young woman on a bench in Bryant Park, across from the New York Public Library. I am sad because my inability to judge character led to my making bad business decisions. This young woman was seeking to make her name in New York and had moved north from Florida. I introduced her to the privileged world of Sea Containers, the parent company of the esteemed hotel and train company then known as Orient-Express Hotels, Trains & Cruises.

I was given a desk in the Sea Containers office at 6th Avenue and 44th Street, near Grand Central Station. And that is how I knew that Sea Containers had an opening for which this composed young lady sitting beside me on the park bench might be suited. Upon my recommendation, she was hired. Within a short time, a talented publicist was hired over her. At this time I realized how much I needed a right-hand person to help me grow Sara Widness Communications. I also needed this person to be closer to the ages of the young people who were cutting their public relations teeth in my company. Knowing how I would feel if someone were hired over me, I invited her to join me in growing Sara Widness Communications. I was sure we could be partners. An attorney drew up papers for us and created a new corporation. This arrangement, finalized with all of the legal i's dotted and t's crossed, involved for her no skin in the game. I didn't know to ask for any skin. And what did I know about hungry young partners? Absolutely nothing. The learning curve was steep and painful.

In the years leading up to 9/11 and before the end of my last New York flyover, Sara Widness Communications in its new iteration was by all definitions hot. Our A-list clients drew the attention of A-list editors and writers. Imagine a card game in which you hold the winning cards. Journalists wanted us, or they wanted what we could offer them: first-class experiences practically anywhere in the world, sybaritic travel at its finest.

At one point we were ten strong, all of the young staff and the junior partner receiving compensation above the norm for entry and mid-level experience in public relations. I was the only person not salaried as I carried the business on my credit cards. To save money I worked on accounts weekends at my dining room table on Staten Island. I was also the office technophobe, exemplified by not one but two computers sitting on my desk. Why? Because I was loathe to give up the old computer when our office system was upgraded. When the staff threatened not to share information with me, my hand was forced to learn the new system on the new computers. I do regret that embracing technology has not been my forte.

In these years my seasonal letters recounted my past year's journeys, until friends and family launched complaints against my good fortune to travel the world. One brother exclaimed: "Sis, you're living the lifestyle of the one percent."

While I may have been tilting toward taking this lifestyle for granted. I never asked for upgrades while booking international flights for journalists whom I escorted around the world. The public relations director of one European airline said she was aware that I never asked for personal privileges. I think she appreciated this. I could always be pleasantly surprised by gestures such as the upgrade to business class that British Airways bestowed on me on one departure.

Shadows

Am I now to be pursued by shadows scavenged,
scuffling over weathered railings on the kitchen porch,
perhaps a rebate gleaned from decades
of scrambled and shuffled lives,
yet surfacing today as monograms
on linens old and yellow that enlivened in tidy piles
other people's hopes in chests, satin stitches here and love knots there,
now tossed into the dust of a flea market
just as the brides, long used up, became dust as the detritus of their lives
lingered to be whitened and mangled into other iterations?

Christmas Staten Island 1997

Packing up. The nagging worry of departure. Lost keys, unwritten
labels, tissue paper lying on the floor ...
I am aware of sadness, of a sense of loss.
— Daphne du Maurier, *Rebecca*

Walking for hours through olive groves above the Ligurian Sea at
St. Fruttuoso and collapsing under a grove splashed with tables
for dining al fresco ... Stunned by Michelangelo at the Sistine Chapel,
tracing with eyes starved for symmetry and grace and color, departing
by necessity ... Dreaming while in Myanmar, some dreams tales of sorrow. I walk with an Asian woman high above the cliffs of the sea. She
falls into a rock-bound pool and drops down, down beyond my grasp.
If I try to rescue her, I, too, drown. She surfaces before she disappears;
at the underwater cave's entrance sits a man, dressed in white, reading.
Bobbi, our guide, says such dreams occur in sequence. An old woman
goes into hospital and exits still sick. I see that she's ill because a nut and
bolt are driven through her heart. She goes back to hospital and emerges
a laughing, dancing boy. I witness from atop a temple in Bagan a herd of
white cattle grazing on the brittle grassy remnants of a deforested river
plain. I take my sunglasses off again and again and look for sweat and
dust. Nothing, then, but blue, shimmering above the backs of the cattle.
Auras, perhaps. At Cape Point in South Africa the Indian and Atlantic
oceans merge... Is this the myth of travel — that our minds become our
own Cape Points and experiences? After many miles, do places and people become one in us?

As we all consciously or not take inventory of a passage of time, I can
say it has been an interesting — and challenging — year.

Black Sunflower Seed

Why this moment
as the sun touches the tulips on the table
do I say your name, forgotten as I write words on the screen
between me and chickadees, stitching who you are
into what will be husks tossed from the feeders
so the scarlet stain that is the cardinal can flourish in the snow.

Time and Takeaways

While I was living on Staten Island and working in Manhattan, time became the ogre in the Grimm fairytale. The monster seven-league boots were always bearing down on me. Saturday mornings were relegated to grocery shopping and visiting the shoemaker, the dry cleaner and whatever other service provider held my life together. At least once and sometimes twice on weekends I would put in more hours at the office, riding the ferry across the water with the promise that after I worked I would take in a foreign film at the Angelika Film Center. As often as not, some weekend hours went to a friend who was an accountant. He helped me unscramble the crazy quilt of paperwork that kept me awake at night. He did this, I think, because he liked me, even understanding that there would be no recompense of any kind. This continued until the company hired a bookkeeper who helped with payroll and tax filings. Although I encouraged my business partner to review accounts with me, she was disinclined to become involved. The business of this expanding company was not her business, a clue I should have picked up on. I was too task-focused.

On Halloween evening of 2002 I was dismantling this office in the landmark Leica Building, on Broadway and Bond, a Manhattan commercial space that I had decked out in a Tuscan gold paint. The arched windows and wooden columns were stripped down to natural wood. My credit card bore the expense of the matching half dozen or more IKEA desks and the ready-made cupboards fronted with panels of a hue that could double as both Scandinavian and Mediterranean blue. The furniture and even the copy machine were headed for the moving van and storage.

That afternoon I stopped by the office of the husband-and-wife team that represented the Leica Gallery. They managed the building that housed our office and may even have owned it. While handing over the keys, Rose (I think that was her name) said not to worry about any moving litter that might be left because the building would take care of everything. That was a relief. Evidently she also knew of the partnership split.

On November 1, 2002, I was on my hands and knees at my house in Barnard, Vermont, poring through cardboard boxes of corporate paperwork that had ridden through the night from Bond Street to the Green Mountains. I was exhausted and in the throes of an oncoming cold. Beside me, also on his hands and knees, was a newly hired accountant whose mission was to review the paperwork in these boxes and prove that I had not, as my former business partner alleged, misappropriated corporate funds. Her letter delivered to the Broadway and Bond office was the final blow in the shattering of our partnership, a shattering that began, or of which I became aware, shortly after 9/11.

I had missed all of her signals. In the summer leading up to 9/11, my partner wanted me to meet some of her close colleagues and family. These included the owner, now deceased, of the White Barn Inn, a prestigious accommodation in Maine whose account she had brought into the company. Another was a man with whom she was friendly, who was unrelated to our partnership but who, in retrospect, may have been providing her advice on how to seize control of the company. The third meeting was over dinner with her mother and stepfather, an accountant. Once she brought into the office a man who was a writer for a well-known magazine. Was he just dropping by to meet me? (Later he joined her staff.) Another arranged meeting was at a hotel consortium gathering, where she introduced me to a few of the key players at Starwood Hotels and Resorts Worldwide, LLC, a subsidiary of Marriott International. In retrospect these meetings paraded me, her business partner, before people who were aligned with her and doubtless supported her strategy to take over the agency and perhaps even to oust me from the company. On another occasion, three or four of our staff were leaving the office allegedly to meet up with a potential client. I suggested joining them. They adamantly refused. The "client" never signed on. What that appointment out of the office was about I'll never know. Suffice it to say that I was being scrutinized and evaluated by my partner, her confidantes, her family and even people within our own office.

I'll hand her this. She knew how to play — and chest — her cards.

Evidently her strategy, which dated from months before, was to stage a palace coup. She had been well advised. On the day the partnership blew up, she froze our corporate bank account and sent letters about the partnership dissolution to clients. Out of the blue that evening, a client telephoned to request that a complete dossier of their information be delivered overnight by FedEx. This was a highly unusual and laden-with-threat demand that gave this client an excuse to cancel its contract the next day because the packet didn't arrive. Other clients followed suit, leaving a shambles of what only days before was one of the most successful boutique public relations companies in New York. In fact, just before 9/11, the company was on target to hit $1 million in revenue. This is the company that I had begun piecing together less than a decade before, when I had found myself with no employment and a new mortgage on Staten Island.

This drama happened out of the blue, or so I perceived then. There had been warning signs. Once I'd heard her say in a disparaging tone, while on a phone call, "just old ladies and gays." This may have been a reference to a 4th of July gathering I'd invited her to on Staten Island, and the "old ladies" (who included me) were in their fifties. And if the office was experiencing a particular crunch, I sometimes called on friends who lived in Manhattan, in their fifties and older, to help us out.

However, the turbulence that followed was most certainly unscripted and something I could never have imagined. One day in January 2002 I asked a staff member to represent the company at a scheduled client meeting out of the office. My request was not out of the ordinary. As an administrator, one of my tasks was to put staff talent where it would best serve the company. Evidently this was the moment the partner had been waiting for, the moment she would shift any balance of perceived power, the moment she could sit on the teeter-totter and leave me, speechless, up in the air with legs dangling. My business partner countermanded my request — in front of the whole staff in our open office. The atmosphere was charged. Mouths all around were agape. Within seconds of back and forth, the partner shouting at me, I requested that she leave the office. We were now near the door. She said, "No, you leave," as she tried to shove me through the door. She left; I stayed. An hour or so later, still shaken, I went out for air, not to return to our still-stunned and very silent staff until later that afternoon. While I was catching my breath, someone in the office found a screwdriver and opened a locked drawer in my desk to remove the corporate checkbook. That night I had the locks on the office door changed.

In this office that was now under siege, belts that were already cinched up in the wake of 9/11 grew tighter as clients dropped like windfall apples. Under the circumstances, little could be salvaged. Clients were disturbed by the very real chaos going on in their public relations company. Some dropped their retainers immediately. One excuse was that they were loyal to each of the partners and therefore could not sustain a contract with either of us. Some staff saw the handwriting on the wall and left; others joined the former partner or sought more stable positions. However, I did not fire anyone.

When the accountant arrived in Barnard on that dismal November 1 day, nearly a year had passed since the office explosion in January. Does it matter how and why it all happened? In retrospect it was just another variation on how people who fail to communicate may fail eventually at whatever their joint undertaking may be. And so I grieved, but not fully until the accountant had sorted the paperwork and until I and my attorney had faced my former partner's tribunal around a huge table in a legal office in Manhattan. At issue was the letter alleging that I had cooked the books.

Eventually, after some $40,000 in accounting and legal bills, I was cleared of any aspersions of wrongdoing concerning the finances of the now defunct company. The process of exoneration dragged on for months while I was managing the termination of contracts on office equipment and leases. She had never bothered to look at the company's accounts. But then, how could she? We didn't have a spread sheet. Whether or not the company was solvent relied on what the bank statements revealed. So why should she bother now with such paraphernalia as IKEA desks and a copy machine?

When the head of the Orient-Express train division in the London office heard of the partnership split, he was heard to say, "That must be a disaster." The devil is in the details. He evidently never knew that it was my stewardship of this account that produced one stunning magazine and newspaper article after another. These successes had nothing to do with my partner. Her own company's website later touted for a time that it was she who had supervised this account.

This hungry young woman had a following like that of a pageant queen or a cheerleader. Men and women alike fell at her feet. Whatever her powers, they have held her in good stead as she reinvented herself as head of her own successful company. The ashes of our failed partnership eventually produced not one but two phoenixes — her company and my rebirth in Vermont.

On Waiting

I waited too long
The weather grew cold
I waited too long
My life became old
I waited too long
The music had died
I waited too long
But finally I cried

The Splintered Galleon

The galleon had splintered. The girl on the prow who gloried in meeting the professional challenges of discerning and demanding clients now had to drag herself to shore. I cannot make light of the distress I felt. However, as shock settled in, a handful of late-arriving takeaways helped to put in perspective how and why things happened as they did.

Health issues can damage the best of intentions. I've always sensed that when people began acting out in untoward ways that they may be on the cusp of becoming ill. Larium, an anti-malarial drug that I took prior to each of two visits to South Africa had undermined my immune system and damaged my health. If I became cranky, which happened, I could always track it to the ever-increasing onslaughts of Larium-induced physical attacks that caused my skin to explode into an eczema-like condition that wept and that caused an extreme fatigue that left my hands shaking and my face drawn and pale. These physical changes could appear within minutes, at unexpected times. At first I thought the condition might be from a disease picked up while traveling in Africa. The tests proved nothing. When I finally was tested for allergies after moving to Vermont, again, nothing showed up that would indicate the kinds of changes my body endured. Then I asked this allergy specialist to look up in his medical compendia conditions related to Larium. Apparently I am one of a hundred who suffer long-term repercussions after taking this potent drug. My system was in constant fight-or-flight mode, which I tried to laugh off. But making jokes about the problem at the office failed to halt the siege on my immune system. My ability to count to ten fell by the way and there was no boundary between me and controlling my emotions.

In a story in the *Guardian*: "Bryce — who had no previous history of illness — suffered what he describes as a 'complete systems collapse.' His symptoms from mefloquine (Larium) included dizziness, fatigue, anxiety and nausea and his vestibular nerve — the part of the brain that controls balance — has now been permanently damaged."

I had these symptoms too, including bouts of depression that I attributed to a round of step aerobics. Another study shows that mefloquine is associated with skin issues. My symptoms appeared as if on cue: a weeping, eczema-like rash behind my ears, on my neck or eyelids. This rash was disfiguring. Years later, one of my daughters told me that my partner confided her concern that my outbursts could lead to my having a stroke. She was probably right. My blood pressure sometimes soared to 190 over something. After all is said and done, perhaps the coup saved my life, even as Larium was destroying my health. I have taken comfort in hearing from two women I mentored while working at the ski resorts years earlier. Each praised my patience with them. I wasn't always under this physical attack. Had I been able to engage differently with the New York team, who knows what the outcome might have been?

Patterns and expectations affect how we live and work. The shoulder-it-all patterns of my life and an inbred fear of confrontation predicted that the partner would have her way. She insisted that we needed more space in which to grow our company. I failed to see that staff members were tripping over each other, competing for computers and desks in our first ad-hoc space. This partner's value to the company's growth called the shots. I was loath to argue with her. When finally I recognized that we had outgrown the office, the monthly office rent for new space tripled, and there were significant expenses for office renovations and furnishings on my credit card.

The staff at this time were young people I had invited first to work with Sara Widness Communications and who then segued into the newly formed company led by the new partnership. They were loyal, despite challenging conditions and my increasing bouts of physical dysfunction. I tried to joke about disfigurements that came on in the space of an hour. My accompanying mood swings were no laughing matter for me or for them.

One young woman made a graceful exit by finding an upwardly mobile niche at a larger public relations company. A young man on the staff became physically aggressive with me one day. I asked our attorney to come by the office the next morning to witness the first firing in the office. Another person declared to a journalist on the phone, within earshot of me (because we were never out of earshot of each other), that she was having a "really shitty day." I confronted her and asked her if she wanted to work at our company. She left.

Our team moved with us from 86th Street and Madison to the new, open-plan offices at Broadway and Bond in lower Manhattan, The partner invited someone she knew to join us. That person brought in a friend from college and so on and so on. The players were talented, bright and excited to be cutting their teeth on public relations in New York City. However, in sharing the hiring powers with my partner, I was also relinquishing control. The newest employees inevitably were allied with the cheerleader-partner who had orchestrated bringing them into the company. Whenever someone new joined us, the partner and I tousled over salary. I always wanted to pay staff higher salaries then she was willing to pay. I do think our entry-level staff earned more money than they would have at similar Manhattan agencies.

As far as my forward-only vision allowed me to see, I saw a team that was collegial and professional. Only one young woman had a short tenure. She paid far more attention to whomever she was instant messaging than to client work. Despite the partner's admonitions that "It's all good!" a bride-to-be planned her wedding at the office, on company time. Her mother-in-law-to-be constantly called. I seemed to be the only person who thought that a wedding should not be planned during business hours. She resigned before the wedding.

Cash flow counts. Credit cards supporting the company were my skin in the game. The partner had no buy-in, which I hadn't thought to request. My credit cards shouldered all of the new office expenses, including rent that had tripled, and these cards picked up the slack when I could not draw salary for myself. Meanwhile the partner insisted she needed more and more and more money. She was the rainmaker; her magnetism drew in new clients. These attributes made her highly valuable to the company's growth. And she was valuable to the staff as well. She provided what I perceived to be a necessary buffer between me, then in my late fifties, and the young people who came into the company. She got the money; I didn't. Cash flow in this under-capitalized enterprise was an issue I hesitated to bring up, even though my money was in this game and hers was not.

Pride goeth before a fall. I prided myself as an ice cutter, always directed forward, looking neither to the right nor to the left, and certainly not behind me. My eyes were focused only on the tasks ahead. And I had no time or inclination to learn what a management training class might have taught me. Time out to pause was time out for sleep. Every minute of every day was scheduled. I had little time to speak on the phone with family and friends. This ice cutter just needed to keep chugging forward, or so I thought. I was dealing not with a little bit of ice, but with icebergs. Management training would have stood me in good stead. At the time of 9/11, with a diminished client base, the belt-tightening worked. The company did not have to lay off anyone. But the sky was getting dark again.

A penny saved is not always a penny earned. An outside accountant prepared the corporate taxes. When I thought we could afford her, eventually a bookkeeper came several times monthly to do our payroll. After all, if I couldn't even draw salary, how could we begin to pay for more attention to the accounting side of things? I thought I could manage cash flow and checkbook oversight by doing due diligence at my dining room table on weekends. The partner declined my offer for her to share in the bookkeeping process. Despite the fact that there were never any spreadsheets to paint a clear picture, I knew in my head all of the scraps of paper that represented receipts, expense accounts and which clients had or had not paid their monthly retainers. A spreadsheet system of painting the financial picture would have saved me $40,000 in accountant and legal fees later on when battling her allegations of malfeasance.

Lavishing praise is huge. As an ice cutter, I seldom took the time to single out staff for their praiseworthy contributions. I expected a lot of myself, had indefatigable energy (except during the increasingly frequent attacks of fatigue induced by Larium and stress) and, consciously or not, I expected everyone to keep up with me. To me it was important they have a livable salary and benefits. Therefore it was heartbreaking to have to cut salaries as clients began to disappear right after 9/11. My intent was to get salaries back on line as the company stabilized. However, the partner failed to see the value in belt-tightening to salvage the company.

In fairness to myself, an epiphany did occur the day I realized it was not the staff's responsibility to understand me. Rather the responsibility was mine to make myself understood. Another epiphany, again staff-related but also with broader implications for clients and business constituents, concerned my self-doubt. Bubbling occasionally to the surface was the idea that I was an impostor on this New York stage. Strangely I never thought this when working at the ski resorts and on the newspapers. Perhaps my make-do Ann Taylor clothes weren't really me. Perhaps the closing-in-on-$400 hair colorings and cuts gnawed at my Puritan roots and weren't really me. Perhaps the manicures undertaken as my last stop before getting to the airport weren't really me. Perhaps the leather purse-cum-briefcase wasn't really me, especially when full of receipts and accounts that I had to sort through.

I understood that others experience distress over similar misapprehensions that they, too, may be impostors. I understood that while there seemed to be something deficient inside me, others perceived me as strong and in charge. My mandate, therefore, was to live up to their image of me, or what I thought that image was. As this practice settled in, I became more comfortable in my own skin — up to a point. Where I failed myself and subsequently others was in my fear of my partner. As she formulated her plot, she became increasingly distant. Only after 9/11 did I begin to suspect that something was afoot. But my ice-cutter focus, looking neither sideways nor behind, didn't allow me to dwell on suspicions. Before the fiasco I was aware that for reasons unknown to me there was a break down in communications. Out-of-office lunches and coffee sessions at Starbucks across the avenue were not affecting what felt to me like a wall between us that was growing higher and higher. I was anxious, as if I were listening to the score of *Jaws*. I had a gut feeling something was wrong.

At this point I arranged to have someone serve as an arbitrator, someone who could help us understand what was happening to the partnership. We again met out of the office, settling in her apartment for a three-way telephone call. Nothing was forthcoming. In retrospect the exercise was like that of dribbling the ball on the basketball court before getting into position to shoot the basket. But by that point, I was afraid of my partner. I didn't know why. I didn't know to ask questions of myself about why she had power over me. Even when encountering those long-ago bosses who fired me, I had never experienced such fear in an office setting or anywhere else. There was something very alive between us that was scary to me.

One assistant stayed on to pick up the pieces of what was left of the business after 9/11 and the insurrection. She told me she suspected something was afoot but didn't know how to tell me.

Busy Bees

Bees, persistent, forage pollen
from particular kinds of flowers,
busy, using more discretion,
than witless men in women's bowers.

Leftover Puritan

While trying to fix cash flow had obsessed me every waking hour in Manhattan and in the preceding years, I had scant time or interest in pursuing a social life. But this did not mean I was living in solitude. Having discovered that the way to a man's heart is not through his stomach, and having wasted years digesting this fact, the birth control pill made possible what over time had become my Herculean quest to probe the mysteries of men's minds, which always held a fascination for me.

Most of these explorations were concentrated in a five-year period right after my divorce. I was still a true-blue wife when I divorced and had never slept with anyone other than my husband. For about ten years after his illness first surfaced, I lived a mostly celibate life. He was mentally ill. And honestly, there's no bigger turn off than the behaviors associated with manic depressive disorder coupled with paranoia and probable schizophrenia. (The new identification for this illness is bipolar. I think this underserves the actual condition. Mania is a very obvious condition, as is depression.)

A few of the men who then crossed my path knew how to converse, which was amusing. Very few had any money, which wasn't. Some were married, which was boring — especially when I met the wives. Several were megalomaniacs, which meant that as long as conversation was only and always about them, they were devoted to me. One plied me with drink at the prestigious New York Yacht Club, to which he belonged, and kissed me in front of the bartender and proceeded to take out the clips holding my hair in a coif and let it loose and admired it, then asked to see me that Saturday. The timing couldn't have been worse. When Saturday came I was just getting over the flu. Because I had scheduled myself — and now him — to participate in some kind of volunteer event on Staten Island, we ate a hasty lunch of tomato soup at my apartment and went to the festivity that had more Norman Rockwell than Manhattan sophisticate to recommend it.

Later, as he puffed his fragrant pipe and drove away in his very nice BMW, sporting his very nice brown tweed jacket, for about two days I suffered twinges of regret over a lost opportunity. I didn't come close to tweed again for several years, until I opened the bed and breakfast in Barnard. Then a guest, a single gentleman, at least for that occasion, parked his Jaguar in my driveway, changed to go to a wedding and left his tweed jacket on a coat hanger in his room. As I freshened his room, I sniffed the weave hungrily.

There were other possibilities: D, with the eating disorder, and M, for whom I didn't have enough time. J had no sense of humor. (That was a huge problem.)

Bottom line: Typical for a member of my generation, for whom repression had been the norm, I was probably on the vanguard of liberated women, even though I never burned my bras. I started taking the pill in 1965 before switching to an IUD. Longing to be emancipated from sexual repression is nothing new. Mary McCarthy wrote about it, based on her Vassar experiences. Enjoying sexual freedom had become a kind of *droit du Señora*. Most illustrious women of history were mistresses many times over. My only problem was that while the men seemed to know how to get what they needed from me, I didn't know how to get what I may have needed from them. I have also surmised that it takes a bloody intelligent and sexy man to keep a warm-blooded woman by the hearth. Bummer. There was never any hearth. Society's dictates and the Ten Commandments work up to a point. Erase society's bondage and there ain't nothing to hold her back, believe me. Wives? My GPS ignored these stop lights.

In my freshman year of college I somehow wandered into the first week of a journalism class that landed me on the college newspaper and into the arms of a senior who was the editor-in-chief. He made poetic overtures to this innocent fresh from a dairy farm in Lowell, Oregon, and I developed an immediate crush on him on our first date. We hobnobbed that night with the student body president and his wife. When I relayed this story to my mother, she commented: "Aren't you flying a little too high and too fast?"

The editor dropped me before Christmas to date a senior who came with all kinds of accolades, including beauty queen. I felt totally diminished. A year later at Christmas he came back into my life and asked me to marry him. He was enlisted in the Army with Reserve Officer Training Corps and was stationed in New Jersey. We didn't see each other again until our wedding in July. Standing with my father before walking down the aisle, I wondered what I was doing. I remember feeling that I was about to make a huge mistake but was powerless to prevent it. I was twenty and, I think, very young. He was twenty-two. We were good companions but not soul mates, and we weren't nurturing. We were both too young and too selfish for that.

Although my husband was an inexperienced lover, we both matured over time. We probably could have grown together into one of those English-type marriages that seem to exist for multiple purposes other than passion, had it not been for his madness. Although some obligatory tears were shed during the futile effort to salvage a marriage with a man who had long since disappeared, my eyes were, for the most part, dry.

If the shedding of tears indicates depth of feeling, then I suspect that through all of my years the only man I was in love with was Joe; but again, he wasn't who he purported to be and couldn't get out of the way of his own secret. Also, after the fact, I have been very hard on myself for investing so much of myself in someone who, through no fault of his own, I know now was incapable of appreciating the me that can write this kind of thing. Not that I ever would have told Joe all of this; but for him I was just a sexual object. He was definitely out of his comfort zone with me. I think we were both uncomfortable to be middle-aged and living in an unmarried state with my two daughters. Even though living together out of wedlock was becoming all the rage, we were still Middle Americans struggling under the albatross of Puritan values.

Some years after Joe's subsequent marriage and his death, I woke with a start one morning. Pieces, as if from a Magritte or Tanguy, fell onto my consciousness. Had he, in fact, owed fealty to another woman, the one who worked in his office and who had a child who was the age a child would have been who might have been conceived on an ill-begotten tryst he had told me about? His allusions to "things not being as they seem" suddenly made sense. How could they be with such a heavy secret that he could never share? When one of his sons called to tell me that his father had married this woman, I cried, evoking the concern of the crew on the Staten Island Ferry I rode to and from Manhattan every day. I have never confirmed my assumptions. Why bother? If validated, they are reason enough to assure me that the secret, and not I, caused our relationship to disintegrate. If not true, my assumptions have given me some degree of comfort. And why demolish comfort?

Another flirtation involved a friend from the Army days. He was charming and witty, and he, his wife, my husband and I were constant companions. My husband and B actually had an affair; her husband and I just lusted. She died of cancer at age forty. This widower and I were like moths around the flame; we could have fallen in love but didn't, because we were extremely combative and competitive. We loved each other on some kind of level but could never have lived together.

D, the man with the eating disorder, deserves to be elucidated because he was quite funny and smart. But he was sad, too, always looking out for the next chance to eat something and more of anything, including rolls slipped off of luncheon trolleys outside the dining room of a swank San Francisco hotel. On a visit to New York he called my office and offered to bring lunch from an eatery called Soup Nazi. I suggested we meet at a nearby café. He brought the soup anyway. We went to the café anyway. While there, he needed to use the restroom. Alas, his portly size posed a challenge as he tried to access this small space. "Ho! Ho! Ho! Sara, I don't fit in the bathroom!" His booming voice thundered to my table. The last I heard of him he was trying to figure out how to get all the leftovers and the soup onto the airplane.

Je ne regrette rien. Each affair has taught me something — about love, about life, about sex, about men, about me.

From 1975 on, the winds of possibility tossed my hair if not my heart. Some encounters were only flirtations; some were outright assignations after the man had plied me with more than one glass of wine; several men were downright safe because they were married. On one hand I knew instinctively not to "fall in love" with a married man. I also knew that I owed no allegiance to the marriage, even though I did not ever want to be destructive. My first-ever lover after I separated from my husband elicited a poem from me about snowflakes falling on my hair. In fact, the white-bound book of poetic scribbles became a diary in iambic pentameter and free verse that summed up more than a few assignations. The man whose affections evidently melted snowflakes was the person I called upon one muggy summer day. In my Volkswagen Beetle I drove through the blinking red light at the four corners in Castleton, Vermont. After taking a direct hit on the driver's side from the other vehicle, which had the right of way, I woke up later at the Rutland Regional Medical Center, where I'd been transported by ambulance. My totaled car went to the junk yard. I couldn't bear to look at it again.

The doctor who examined me said he had been dealing with accidents all day because of the low oxygen level in the air. He released me. I called the only person I knew who lived in Rutland, the snowflake boy, who drove me back to the East Poultney General Store. Here shock set in and I sobbed and shook for what seemed hours. The doctor hadn't prepared me for this.

On another occasion I was driving my Saab one morning on the way to my office on the mountain. This was my second used Saab. Both were the funky, sort-of-ugly models that screamed to my out-of-the-box tastes. They also had rack and pinion steering. This feature translated to a remarkable fortitude when taking curves at very high speeds. On this morning I was on a straightaway when the car stopped, literally dead in its tracks. The engine block had fallen from the car, halting all progress. This incident forced me to conclude that I would be best served with a brand-new car. Help was on its way as Le Car, Renault's equivalent of a sardine tin on wheels, but minus the wind-up key, had just hit the Rutland market and was affordable. The first time the car and I together climbed the steeps to my office, Le Car began to signal distress. So did I until someone explained that there was a cooling mechanism in effect because Le Car was overheated. So was I.

Another man, single and wealthy, wanted me in his life, but when he told me, "You look lovely in my dining room," I felt like one of his collector plates on the wall. The only reason that comes to mind today for this extreme reaction to the compliment was the possibility of being committed to someone for whom I had no affinity, despite the fact that he could have provided security for me and my daughters. Yet another might-have-been suitor had some potential until he told me about his fetish of wearing women's nylons. Hah! He should have worked in New York and commuted by subway in the hot summer months. That would have put an end to that eccentricity.

After playing footsies with me at a ski writers' meeting, a bachelor, divorced, professed to be in love with me, spent Christmas with me and my daughters, then didn't call for a week. When his call came, he told me he was getting married. He had roots in Norway. Maybe it was the finnan haddie I'd served for Christmas breakfast. Another flirtation was already married; this friendship went on for several years, but after dining with his family, I had to move on. And yet another married rogue, who'd been schooled by the Jesuits, wiggled his way through his dual life through a logic only the Jesuits understand. We had a lot of fun: theater, opera and travel. I think we enjoyed each other's company and we laughed a lot. He had a remarkable oddity. Now, haunting thrift shops isn't odd. Scavenging thrift shops in Westchester County for designer garments to gift to a friend borders on odd. Bringing the gifts in a shopping cart scarfed from a nearby grocery store near Union Square to my office door is definitely odd.

Right after 9/11, out of the blue, a man from my high school past reached out to me. He was a year ahead of me in the small rural school where we both led our classes academically. I remember dancing once with him at an Honor Society party, but we never dated. He told me he was afraid that my mother would object to my dating him. This was the country. There were no tracks to be on the other side of. He perceived there were. This kind and gentle man helped me through the post 9/11 shock that New Yorkers experienced, and then through the dissolution of my hard-earned company. After giving Manhattan the better part of a year after these debacles, I wondered why I was floundering in my half-empty office stripped necessarily of staff because I could no longer pay them. Well into my sixty-second year, I had no will or resources to rebuild a business that had given me pleasure — and now heartache.

However, the tide was on the turn.

My destination on Halloween when a moving van came to Broadway and Bond to collect office furniture and equipment was Barnard, Vermont, where in 1998 I had had the foresight to purchase a house that subsequently was renovated to become the Fan House Bed & Breakfast. This dwelling was always known as the Fan House, so named because of architectural embellishments that resemble fans placed above all the windows. They also resemble half-moons, so I suppose it could also be called the Half-Moon House. Though I toyed with such romantic names as Innisfree, my marketing instincts came to the fore to remind me that the house was already branded the Fan House, so I should leave the name alone. The old school friend continued to support me with phone calls and emails, and I discovered a world of caring from the heart and mind that had no connection whatsoever to a physical presence. Quite simply, he brought joy into my life, as well as creativity and hope.

Before They Needed Dreams

Let her have her dreams then.
They're of an old man who wasn't always so.
She, like he, wasn't always old.
Too, he says, he dreams of her,
both recalling youth
before they needed dreams.

Road Less Traveled

May 5, 2004, on the Appalachian Trail in Barnard, Vermont: The loveliest walk through the woods today ... A friend and I began our hike on the Appalachian Trail just off Route 12 between the Fan House and Woodstock. The climb was fairly precipitous and strenuous, with me setting the pace because I can't stand to be behind people who walk at a pace slower than I mine. Short zigzags up through the mix of evergreens and deciduous trees, with yellow dogtooth and white violets along a trail that moved into beech glades with a few maples tossed in, leaves just beginning to come out; a pond down to the right; freshets here and there.

The trail became flirty, tracing the west-facing slope at a horizontal, providing some relief from the uphill, before turning gently up again and scissoring the slope, slicing to a northeasterly direction. We passed a magnificent stand of birches, with two stately old trees that looked like the mothers of all birches. Then straight up to the most expansive meadowland — with views, I believe, in every direction but north/northwest, showcasing the undulating hills here that are in such an intimate, human scale.

We climbed over an old-fashioned stile, following the path back into the woods, a level terrain with sweet pink flowers along the trail and the cry of an owl that two fellows farther up trail spotted and said had a huge wing span. One of the men had done work on my house and he remembered me as the lady who was the first to swim in the lake two summers ago (my polar bear year). We chatted for a while; continued on, spotting trillium, spotted adder (a yellow lily-like flower), delicate edelweiss-type blossoms (may have been bloodroot) and purple violets. We then passed by a felled birch whose bark had turned silver. Ahead, up a slight incline, were moss-covered stones, vestiges of an old hearth and chimney. Glades traversed by rivulets flowed in front.

We walked through what seemed to be (but probably wasn't) a primal forest of evergreens, where passage became slippery because of the needles underfoot. At one point the trail was so level and inviting I started jogging or lightly running. The sense of freedom and happiness this environment inspires is beyond words. Songbirds sang at the tops of deciduous trees or gamboled through the evergreens. Fresh chips on one tree indicated that a woodpecker had been quite busy. There were a few places where the trail became a bit difficult to follow, but if we looked carefully, we could recover it, or at least see the white trail markings on a tree up ahead. We came down off the trail right where the car was parked, ambled across a little footbridge, where signs said two miles to such-and-such a point on the trail and nearly seven to another, and we vowed to make that one another outing. In all, we had hiked for ninety minutes and it was like a week's vacation.

From the Gardens of Confucius

From the nest babies perch
on five-hundred-year-old limbs,
like China's children
poised to fly from their own branches.
Note: birds are white called Lusi

Eighty years ago the girls' feet grew small.
Today the feet of China's girls stretch beyond the walls.
Castanets of a thousand cicadas in the cedars
surround Confucius and his guests.
Note: cedars reflect longevity

Sorting the Future

With the love and emotional support my school friend brought into my life, I found the strength to begin sorting out what was next.

In the summer of 2002, immediately after the double whammy of 9/11 and the company's dissolution, I had an opportunity to travel to China to teach English in a Chinese boarding school. My compensation would be to tour China for six weeks. Getting as far away from my reality at the time seemed like a good thing to do. While traveling, I left what remained of my public relations company in the capable hands of my younger daughter.

Over the years I have become accustomed to sybaritic travel. My work requires taking journalists to elegant hotels and resorts, work that is cushioned by expense accounts and hovering hosts. So imagine the surprises of a six-week foray to China this summer to teach English to Chinese youngsters — an adventure laden with flies, probably fleas, grain-stuffed pillows, kids who spit in the classroom and bad chalk.

Forewarned that this would be a difficult journey, the only concessions to *haute* that tagged along were my expensive backpack on wheels and a black leather carry-on embossed with a client's emblem. This carry-on, a client's gift to me for good work done the previous year, was to become a reminder of my past life. A fax for me arrived at China's New Century School advising that one of the last of my clients was withdrawing from my life, perhaps because I went so far away — or down market?

The initial premise of the trip, as organized by a Chinese-American woman with altruistic ties to her homeland, was that a group of twelve Americans would travel for just over a month on buses full of middle-school youngsters. The Americans could explore China while helping the kids hone their English as they began a several-year preparation targeted at training them to become hosts of the 2008 Olympics.

However, the best laid plans for this travel and, it would become clear, for my life immediately went awry. Upon our arrival in Beijing and after our first night of sleeping on grain-filled pillows, three of us were immediately siphoned off from our group and assigned to teach in Heze (formerly Caozhou) is in Shandong Province, southeast of Beijing, far away from tourist sites but very close to kids.

The remainder of the group would tour for two weeks and then replace us while we toured. Quid pro quo. We would teach for two weeks and, as compensation, tour China, compliments of the government. Turns out that this was a monetary transaction with Heze's New Century School that paid a bounty for our heads to a Chinese tour operator. Mr. Lee stretched his budget amongst us as far as it would go. And he neglected to advise us, before we left North America with airline tickets we had paid for, that the intent of the program had changed.

Here's what happened. We had been told that we would ride a bus with young Chinese selected to be hosts for the upcoming Olympic Games. We would help them polish their English with this world event in sight. Chinese lore is big on ghosts. And that's what the Olympic host hopefuls and an extended bus tour with the kids became to the three of us who were assigned to the school. We established a routine in Heze that included five hours of teaching, Monday through Saturday. There were always three daily cafeteria-style meals, each with at minimum three green vegetables, sometimes with eggs and rice, depending on the time of day. We each had a roommate. Mine was a Beijing University girl, assigned to smooth our way, who referenced Mao in reverent terms while dreaming of leaving China.

Heze days fell into a pattern of my early rising, perhaps spending a few minutes looking out the barred (against what?) seventh-story window of the dorm room in the New Century School. The view was of cement and cinder-block dwellings, replete with winged roof spirits, and a dusty path that led to a canal with a solid surface of garbage. Heze days were hazy, with a blood-red sun infrequently breaking through the pollution.

From the New Century School I watched a woman walk with a dog in her arms through the banners hung from the winged portal, red cloths tinged with yellow, signifying something. The portal, perhaps twenty feet high, of brick, looked like a child's rendering, with a roof stroked to a curve, in brown tiles. At the top of the roof were statues, perhaps a foot high, balanced on the ridgeline, a motif of spirits repeated on some but not all of the two-story, shed-like dwellings of yellow brick or cinder block. From the horizon, these tiled roofs looked like swaths of plowed fields in chocolate brown, russet and occasionally orange-red.

An alley that was colored from the same pigment as the ochre-washed buildings stretched past the electric poles to the scholar trees that lined the river, perhaps a half-mile away. Between clusters of dwellings was green grass with a path over there off the alley's dust. Some of the houses had canopies over the two or three windows that faced the morning sun, giving them heavy lids of aqua, green and marine blue.

Five people, children and adults, were down there in that courtyard behind the bannered portico, one of them sweeping the dust, the man squatting before a red plastic basin, now washing his face. He went to the clothesline and pulled off a cloth and wiped himself before tossing the cloth behind him, back onto the line. A woman pulled a blue shirt over a child's head. Behind this brick wall, day had begun in Heze, land of peonies.

Reading about China in fact and fiction became part of the routine. An understanding of the world's most populous, 6,000-year-old culture began to emerge. This reading was competed with the self-imposed "lights out" at 9 p.m., as my roommate watched her favorite television programs from Japan, translated into Chinese.

There was something bordering on excitement as we daily witnessed the progress of a road outside New Century School. In two weeks this road was transformed, going from two feet of cement-colored dust upon our arrival to dust suffused with water to wet dust covered with hay and plastic to compact it. Eventually some kind of black surface was applied. Most of this effort took place with scant benefit of heavy equipment as bicycles and vegetable carts skimmed across the dust.

I and my young American companions felt something resembling accomplishment as we daily imposed on the headmaster, who had a car, to drive us through the dust to a hotel in Heze. At the hotel the bartender translated our three-fingers signal and poured us each a glass of red wine. We three then commiserated over our lack of materials to work with, the spitting kids and bad chalk. We wove in victories that were our daily due: students who used prepositions correctly or who sang a song in English or who learned to "think out of the box" while writing an essay on "my life as a mountain" after pondering the assignment for thirty minutes. It appeared that their creative sides had never before been challenged — at least in English — at school.

For me there was something bordering on contentment in being away from clients, business worries and the electronic world. However, accessing the computer in the headmaster's office revealed that I might be justified in my worries over business, as problems back at the office had multiplied. Remember that curt memo faxed to me in China, all the way from the UK, from the client that had gifted the leather travel bag to me the year before? Was the client firing me from their account because I was too far away from client concerns?

Excitement? Accomplishment? Contentment?

For the first time in years my focus was on people — not tasks; on faces — not machines; on communication — not reports; on children — not clients.

However, just as with many Chinese with whom I interacted at New Century School and while traveling, I felt new urges to assume a more liberated stance, to distance myself from ways of being that posit tasks, reports, machines and clients as more important than people, faces, communication and children.

If achieving this freedom meant climbing seven flights of steps several times a day because New Century School's elevator had shut down to conserve energy, or wishing with the students that the sun would break through the fossil-fuel-imposed tarnish, or squatting over hole-in-the-ground latrines, or performing for two weeks with nary an English book in sight, then China's New Century School accomplished what a vacation is supposed to.

If achieving this freedom meant conducting a New England–style "town meeting" in a Heze classroom to demonstrate a new way of decision-making, or receiving the kids' kudos for singing American songs in an impromptu karaoke evening, or being part of the school's finale, during which students played ancient Chinese instruments and demonstrated their mastery, in English, of an Ibsen sketch, then China's New Century School accomplished what a vacation's supposed to.

I had gained a new grip on reality. This reality became even more profound as I gripped my embossed, black leather carry-on, that vestige of sybaritic travel, and checked myself into the Art Deco world of Shanghai. I ensconced myself in the Peace Hotel on the Bund for two nights before my journey home. At night I dined lavishly on French cuisine in the formal dining room overlooking the lights of Shanghai.

When the Wool Gets Pulled

Just poor little lambs doing what we oughta.
We're poor little lambs going off to slaughter.
Signs of death are all about us
but our wool's so thick
we can't see the bus.
Just poor little lambs
with a noose around each neck,
poor little lambs
in the middle of a wreck.

Too Heavy to Carry

This simulated-leather carry-on, or "weekender," when packed, is too heavy for me to carry because it has no wheels. It sits unused in my bedroom closet in Barnard, Vermont. Did the London office of Orient-Express Hotels, Trains & Cruises know when they gifted this carry-on to me that a year later they would dismiss me as their consultant? Was there yet another hungry public relations consultant waiting in the wings and promising the company grander results than I had brought to them? Or was the gift simply a gesture of gratitude for having escorted countless journalists around the world on their behalf? I can only say that this duty was my pleasure while riding the rails on the Venice Simplon-Orient-Express in Europe, and while on a similar short-lived luxury train down Australia's coast, and while peering through the windows from Singapore to Bangkok on the Eastern & Oriental Express. A deluxe riverboat, *Road to Mandalay*, opened my eyes to Burmese culture. Countless luxury hotels welcomed me with flourishes that extended from long-stemmed roses (in such profusion that I stopped counting them) in rooms overlooking the Grand Canal to an invitation to stay in the Copacabana Palace's presidential suite, with its view of Copacabana Beach in Rio de Janeiro. I was driven through orange and cork trees, along with vineyards, en route from Lisbon to the Algarve; I swam under Table Mountain at the Mount Nelson in Cape Town; I had tea on an expense account at the Ritz in London. Shall I continue?

General managers in these arenas of rarefied air are impeccable hosts. Those with whom I was privileged to work were cultivated, fluent in several languages and always gracious. That I wasn't a film star or Nancy Reagan made no difference. I and my media entourages were always treated like royalty while staying in the hotels and while touring regions as guests of these establishments. The late Hans Stern, whose name is embellished on fine jewelry stores throughout the world, made his yacht available to me and my guests when we were in Rio de Janeiro. He always made a point of personally welcoming my media guests when we toured his heavily guarded workshop and sales rooms in Rio. Then he would ask me into his office for a chat. Once he gifted me with a book that was important to him — a book on the Holocaust. A poem on this subject I shared with him elicited the following note:

> *Dear Ms. Widness,*
> *With pleasure I read your message and the touching poem you wrote. Unfortunately, the sense of fear you mentioned hovers above everyone's mind. Let us hope the world will be in a better situation soon. I wish you good luck for your new projects, and I hope we will see each other again, either here or in New York. You know that I am very fond of you.*
> *Best regards, Hans Stern*

Even a very disagreeable food-and-beverage manager failed to lessen my enthusiasm for the Carlyle in Manhattan (the New York equivalent of the hotels I represented, which have since been rebranded from Orient-Express Hotels to Belmond). I was a relative newcomer to Manhattan and definitely new to the world of the elite. I wore a dress one day when meeting with this manager, and he didn't like it; the dress obviously was off the rack and not couture. Unused to being yelled at, I immediately sought the counsel of another, very kind manager at the hotel. I was kept on this account, but thankfully I never met with the angry man again. And I don't recall wearing that dress again in Manhattan.

Dressing for success at such a level was an issue. In previous lives I had been accustomed to making my own clothes and as a seamstress had advanced to couture status. Manhattan's Lower East Side was a treasure trove of fabrics. One store carried the ends of bolts used in couturier fashions. However, as engaged as I was in my demanding consulting work, I had no time for sewing the clothes that would have been so useful to me now. I had always preferred working with the patterns that Yves Saint Laurent designed for Vogue Patterns. In ready wear, Ann Taylor served my wardrobe needs for a few years. As my figure grew "more womanly," as one daughter likes to say, I discovered Marina Rinaldi, an Italian designer whose early lines were exquisite. Twice a year I would call this shop on Madison Avenue and ask if one particular member of the staff could give me one hour on a certain day. She had an uncanny ability to select what I would like. The garments I chose were of natural fabrics, elegantly designed and impeccably tailored. This was as close as I could afford to come to couture.

Also on my favorite avenue were shops that carried once-worn designer garments. Pucci became a particular favorite. My wardrobe needs were complicated; I needed clothes to suit climates from Manhattan to Europe, including Mediterranean and tropical. A few favorite silk and linen pieces were always running the circuit between my suitcases and the dry cleaners on Staten Island. Packing was never a chore.

Assembling my champagne-chic wardrobe on a beer budget also required that I wear black and look as thin and as young as possible for weekly meetings with the Miramax Films team at their offices in Lower Manhattan. This independent film company set the mark for what are known as "indies." Miramax hired me to get their movies recognized beyond the film pages. The young twenty-something women assembled around the table all seemed to wear size two Versace. I lived in horror of their ever discovering that I was a new grandmother. Packaging coupled with at least a dollop of talent is the survive-in-Manhattan formula. Fortunately, youthful genes worked to my advantage for many years and I wasn't "the old lady" yet.

Even in Manhattan, remaining undiscovered or undercover wasn't easy. This proved true in the case of one Miramax movie I worked on. Perhaps the most exciting campaign I waged was for the movie *Priest*. This film addressed the realities of the sexual lives of some priests. The controversy around this subject was, of course, anticipated. But Disney (in charge of its release) added fuel to the fire by planning to open it in theaters on Good Friday. This fact drew the ire of the Catholic League who called a press conference in New York to air their annoyance. The opening subsequently was rescheduled; but in the meantime the movie had garnered national attention thanks to the film's delicate subject. I was directed to assemble Manhattan's religious leaders, including the moral advisor to the Cardinal of the Archdiocese of New York, in one room to discuss the film. This gathering was followed by a press conference organized by the Catholic League, whose members were irate. I was a mouse in the audience for this conference. However, the owners of the dry cleaners on Staten Island saw me on television as cameras panned the audience; they told me so the next time I brought in my linens and silks to be dry cleaned. To this day, I think the wife suspected I was a "mole" and I began fearing for the safety of my garments. The Catholic League press conference was followed by a second press conference at the request of Miramax and Disney to announce that the release date had been changed. Local and national networks turned out. That *Priest* would make the headlines was a given.

Hostility to this film brought at least one bomb threat to the Miramax office. I made every effort to accomplish the work laid out for my team, but we flew under the radar. I didn't want to put my staff at risk at our unsecured office at 86th and Madison.

My small company had a four-year run with Miramax when the Weinstein brothers were championing independent films. Then Disney took over the company, and the public relations and marketing machine changed. This change had already begun with *Priest*. On campaigns preceding *Priest* I was successful in getting press placements in travel sections of newspapers for these films, among others: *A Month by the Lake, Enchanted April, Muriel's Wedding* and *Passion Fish*. Travel sections were not normally home to movie items. *Ready to Wear* (original title: *Prêt-à-Porter*) showed up on fashion pages. *Like Water for Chocolate* made the culinary columns after my office ran a national search for the most seductive chocolate recipe. When a small box arrived one day at my office, I knew the campaign was successful, although the contents of the box, a replica of a female breast molded in white chocolate, didn't win a prize. Nor did we taste it. *Il Postino* drew writers to comment on poetry readings my team had arranged in bookstores around the country. The litany of movies that jumped into other sections of newspapers and magazines goes on.

This work was fun and demanding, and it required an urgency that, in retrospect, made promoting a ski season look like child's play. From start to finish, we had perhaps one month to make a film a box office winner by using out-of-the-box guerrilla tactics. I was being well compensated for my creativity, perhaps for the first time in my life. In the end, the creative mentality I applied to the world of film promotion was no different from the creative mentality that had gone into the "ding-dong tapes," which had been mocked in the highly conservative environment of the ski resort not so many years before. This new world known as Miramax in which I moved for nearly four years was the antithesis of conservative — except for the size two Versaces.

Shadows of Their Lives

Again I return to the carpet by the stairs,
staring down into time to reach weavers
threading weft and woof
with skeins of earth-tone wool
in villages that history stained with blood
until "rich in history" became a place that people had to flee,
leaving worn rugs, shadows of their lives,
on which I tread.

Sheets in the Wind

The idea for a working title for this book, *From the Carlyle to the Clothesline,* or *I Used to Have More Fun Between the Sheets,* came as an epiphany one day when I was standing between lines of damp, white sheets, affixing them with clothespins to the clotheslines so the linens would take as little space as possible. When you triple-sheet a bed you use three sheets at a time, not just two. The two top sheets with the blanket in between create a blanket sandwich that keeps the blanket clean. Multiply three sheets times three rooms. Toss in mattress pads and liners, pillowcases and pillow liners. A full-house turnover, re-doing each guest room from scratch, adds up to a hefty amount of laundry to be blown about on a nice day.

I am wrestling one sheet after another onto the lines, watching out of the corner of my eye as a few that are already beginning to dry threaten to fly away in the gusts of wind. Before I moved to Barnard did I have more fun between the sheets? No. Although the thread count at the Carlyle was in the stratosphere, my carefully curated, six-hundred-plus-thread-count linens are as white as the sun can bleach them and smell as sweet and fresh as the meadows around my house. Is doing all of this laundry over and over and over again fun? No. But guests love the Fan House and especially my high thread-count linens, and I love making an environment pleasurable for people.

Purchasing this 1840s village house in Barnard was possible because the woman who sold the house to me is a friend. I enjoyed weekends in her home. I always remarked that I had the best sleeps of my life here. Vermont was as old and comfortable as this house. I asked the owner to give me right of first refusal should she ever want to sell. She did, and the rest, as they say, is history.

In the tradition of cottages of yesteryear, every inch of floor and molding was painted. A young friend moved up temporarily from Manhattan to camp out here as the official stripper. In some swaths of woodwork the original milk paint refused to budge. That patina gives the décor the visage of an attractive elderly lady whose face powder shimmers over aging cheekbones.

After the house was literally jacked up on what looked like large Lincoln logs in order to pour a concrete basement, the already-cracking plaster walls began to crumble. As the repairs were made, the plasterer and I marveled at the horsehair structure of plaster splayed on lathe. While the walls may contain secrets, none was discovered during reconstruction.

The late Roger Webster, a local Barnard legend, was the contractor who plied the underbelly of the house with a Lincoln-log lattice. We needed elevate it high enough to get earth-moving equipment underneath, in order to pour the basement. While the house was airborne, Roger suggested that I might not want to come up from New York, as in his experience homeowners became very anxious upon seeing their house hobbled this way. So I didn't. And I also wasn't around when he suggested that my barn, covered with old-fashioned, hand-split wooden shakes, needed to come down because it was unstable, thanks to a direct lightning hit. At my suggestion, he agreed to take the structurally challenged barn half down. When he called me one evening to report on his crew's progress, he said: "Well, the good news is that the barn is down. The bad news is that it is all down." Houses of cards have a way of resisting best intentions. But after this and the house elevation, I gained new appreciation for a language that includes with identical pronunciations but opposite meanings. You can have a barn or house raising and also a razing.

Out of the razing that I missed came early paintings of William B. Hoyt, an artist who had lived in the Fan House in the 1970s. I brought his paintings into the house for safe-keeping, selected three that I especially liked and placed them about. When I called the artist and asked if he would please come collect his work, he came and saw that I was enjoying some of his art and left these three for me. I hope he hasn't regretted his decision. Among his circle of friends is an artist from Australia who stayed at the Fan House. I am fortunate to own a painting of Judy Garb Weiss. This work, which I call *Chicken Lady*, resides in my dining room below a painting of a pair of pears purchased from Crate & Barrel.

Working with an artifact — this house — that predates me by some one hundred years requires direct communication. I am not of a New Age bent, but I did speak with the house along the refurbishment route, asking the house what it would like me to do. This strategy, I think, prevented me from making something too perfect of this antique. For efficiency's sake the windows need to be replaced, but that can wait as a task for the next steward.

Furnishing the Fan House was the fun part. Although I incline to Shaker minimalism, guests prefer a softer, warmer environment. My intended palette included Mediterranean blue. Alas, the northern light of Vermont is wan at best except for a few weeks in late August, when around six o'clock in the evening the sun, just before falling behind the ridge called the Chateauguay, strikes the garden with an effervescence I call the fairy light. Colors and shapes waver in the temptation to disappear into its magic — best experienced with a glass of wine in hand, of course. All by way of saying that the light here is prejudiced toward earth tones. Thus the natural wood of moldings and floors became the inspiration for golds and russets and a liberal application of carpets.

How easy it would have been to tumble into a themed environment. I have always disliked Victoriana, so I wasn't at risk of trending in that direction. Big and over-stuffed pieces of clubby furniture are too massive for the rooms (as, occasionally, are the guests). A loose translation of Mediterranean finally emerged, with just enough but not too much toile. The décor displays either ignorance or fearlessness, a mix of square-nail rustic farm pieces and batik foraged from Arab Street in Singapore along with hand-loomed linens from Myanmar (Burma), once displayed by merchants high above the Irrawaddy River at Mandalay.

I had always wanted in my house a sofa that was deep enough to sink into while allowing a height-challenged person to sit without feet dangling in the air. A professional decorator sourced the perfect pair of love seats for the living room. She also provided fabric swatches to dress the bedrooms. The scheme we worked out together has worn well, over two decades later. I lost touch with her, but not before she had told me her story. Still in high school, she became pregnant. Her parents sent her to a home for unwed mothers. She was forced to put the baby up for adoption. End of child, end of family of origin, end of story. Trauma still stalks her. Her story is now buried in the generous arms — walls — of the Fan House, walls that have absorbed many joys and sorrows over time.

The Blue Shell

We hold each other cupped in the palm
as a child cherishes the orphaned robin's egg,
yet distressed to leave intact this perfect azure sphere.
Curious, fragile, we see clear repercussions
of probing too close this thin, blue shell.

Ghost Roster

As steward of a house that is nearly two hundred years old, I can make only one promise. The only resident ghost, a little girl I dubbed Molly, left years ago. She was around for some time after I moved in, according to one of my daughters and to occasional visitors, including an au pair who claimed she saw Molly coming up the stairs dressed in a white frock and wearing a bonnet trimmed with a red flower. Sometimes visiting dogs would refuse to go upstairs with their owners. I never experienced Molly until a day I was standing at the kitchen sink and I felt a rush past my left cheek, as if a cold kiss had been planted there. I thought I was alone in the house. The evidence was out of the box. Molly had been living in the Fan House, but she had for her own reasons just kissed me goodbye. I like to think she was satisfied with how her domicile was being treated. She hasn't returned.

While she was living here, I preferred not to share her presence with my guests. I didn't want the house to have the reputation of being haunted. One day, however, a grandmother was visiting with her teenage granddaughter, both from Texas. I thought it might be fun to share the story of Molly. All went well until breakfast the next morning when the grandmother glared at me. Although they had separate bedrooms, her granddaughter was so frightened she had moved into her grandmother's bed for the duration. (Maybe together they are still enjoying the story.) Another guest woke up on another night to find her bed shaking. She came downstairs petrified. I wish I knew then what I know now. Small earthquakes strong enough to shake beds sometimes strike Vermont.

Since early 2003, when the doors of the Fan House officially opened to paying guests, I've received visitors from as far away as Sri Lanka and Indonesia. The Sri Lankan announced upon arrival with his lovely blonde Canadian companion, who sported a vivid black eye, that he was a Tamil Tiger. I concerned myself before their departure over what I would do were he to show his stripes under my roof. Fortunately he did not.

I had a full-house takeover on the night I donated rooms to members of a local arts council who were hosting the Tuvan Throat Singers. On a tour of the United States, these men were straight out of southern Siberia, on the border of Mongolia. The Fan House was responsible for lodging the eight guests and serving breakfast the next day. I researched what they might prefer for breakfast, and a day or two in advance of their arrival the kitchen reeked of lamb bones boiling on the stove. This broth, with bread, would be their breakfast. They ate heartily and as a thank you performed a short concert at the house that evening.

Another intriguing guest was the woman wearing too much lipstick who arrived down the driveway in a car with no license plates. Because I do not take credit cards, I confess to having concerns on a few occasions that the gentlemen's agreement to pay by cash or personal check upon departure will not be honored. This guest evoked that concern. As I do on infrequent occasions, I surreptitiously write down a license plate number — just in case. However, her car offered nothing. She did pay, after disappearing to somewhere in the vicinity, doubtless to collect her due, and I was surprised to get a Christmas card from her that year. The card was a picture of her in a provocative pose. A few other guests have forgotten to bring their checkbooks or to get cash from a bank machine, on which occasions I whisk off my apron and arrange to follow them to a bank in Woodstock or Bethel so as not to inconvenience them by asking that they return to the house after a cash machine transaction.

My steepest learning curve at the Fan House was learning to ask for money. This I do when a booking is made. I decided early on not to take credit cards. Rather, payment comes in the form of a check in advance of arrival. However, sometimes a last-minute booking requires guests to pay upon arrival. Dealing in tender that is exchanged so personally, *mano a mano*, was a hurdle. These are very different transactions measured in several hundreds of dollars instead of the thousands I had been used to handling when running the public relations business. I chose not to use credit cards for several reasons. When a reservation is made, it's usually done on the phone. I hear a voice; I take down details about what they prefer for breakfast. They then send a check that usually arrives tucked in a note card, often from a museum. Credit cards and what's known as online booking do away with these personal interactions. By the time someone arrives here, I have a sense of their aesthetic taste, their handwriting and their civility, because they usually write a nice note. However, I soon lost any trepidation about asking for money. Also lost along the way was my feeling responsible if a new guest glowered coming through the door, as did the Romanian with his lovely British wife and two daughters. The fact that he glared daggers when I welcomed them had nothing to do with me and probably everything to do with the fact that I reminded him of his primary school teacher in his former Communist dictatorship.

Once in a great while a couple, always older, will appear who evidence no vestiges of why they ever got together in the first place. They reveal themselves quickly. A wife interrupts everything her husband says, perhaps because she's heard his stories one too many times. The husband shows no deference to his wife when coming to the dining room. Sitting at the table hunched over his plate, he starts shoveling. I remember on one occasion such a guest left the table beaming, because I had just brought in more and more food. He loved my pancakes.

Such negative experiences are few and far between. While the house is far from rustic, there are no televisions or individual thermostats in guest rooms, no his-and-hers sinks. In one bedroom guests bump their heads on a dormer getting in and out of bed. Well-traveled guests focus not on deficiencies but instead on an ambiance they refer to time and again as "European" or "Italian." I credit the Fan House for drawing A-list guests who, except when the wind blows and they don't heed my advice to dress warmly for inside as well as out, are charming and courteous as they convey the outside world to me.

The night before one of the first guests of the Fan House checked in, friends sat around after dinner talking about how one carries on a conversation with total strangers to whom the intimacy of your home is being offered. All agreed that race, religion and politics — the golden oldies — would be off limits, giving scant attention to what today's specific no-no's might be.

One couple arrived at the door midafternoon on a Friday in mid-October 2003, in time for the rehearsal for the wedding over which he would preside on Saturday. I asked if they would like tea, coffee, wine or scotch upon their return that evening. He replied "Scotch" and I immediately pegged him as Episcopalian, a fact confirmed when he sipped his Scotch in front of the fire that evening and asked the room — myself, house guests and his wife: "Well, who thinks we should invade Iraq?" We all looked at each other. Eventually the reverend's wife interjected her thoughts, noting that she had never had a chance to discuss this issue with her husband before.

A young couple who loved the house spent one day exploring the nooks and crannies of the region but somehow didn't seem excited by the prospect of a second day delving into the area's commercial outlets, which are charming but limited. I asked if they liked to hike; they said yes. So I invited them to join me on a swath of the Appalachian Trail that extends over a ridge six miles from the house. Some ninety minutes later we exited the trail, slightly damper for wear but exhilarated, and I thought, *What a memory this is compared to a souvenir.*

One couple, both healers, were visitors a few days after I had broken my little finger while brushing two golden retrievers. I sat on my finger when one of the dogs knocked me over. The wife suggested that they do a healing for me, if I were willing. I sat in front of the fire with one hand atop the other as her husband in the background and she in front of me closed their eyes and moved their hands across an energy field.

After a while, I had the sense of the injured hand levitating and opened my own eyes to witness that it indeed had risen. As this was happening there was a distinct movement and pain with the injured finger. After an hour the session was concluded. She called a few days later and I told her that what I had asked for — a way of healing the finger without a large cast — had been accomplished. The doctor took one look at the finger, looked at the x-rays and said he had been prepared for surgery but it looked as if the finger was already straightening itself out. A few turns of tape around a finger-sized "shell" to keep it stable was all that was required.

Another broken bone didn't heal as easily. I was with a young visitor, crossing a frozen river near the house. Instead of walking with snow-shoes on the ice I opted to belly across the river on a snow-covered log. I slipped and the next thing I knew my wrist was being snapped back into place at the local hospital.

Ode to the Fireplace Suite

If you want to freeze your tuchus be my guest.
If you want to have a fire as you rest,
you will find the linens luscious
and the Fan House breakfast scrumptious.
If you want to freeze your tuchus be my guest.
I warn you to bring clothing fit for cold.
You arrogantly think that's just for old,
that to garb yourself for zero
would make you less than hero.
If you want to freeze your tuchus be my guest.

Collectibles

A Barnard neighbor stopped by to tell me that a long-time friend had resurfaced in his life. She'd had a very bad car accident and her head had been repeatedly slammed as her pickup truck rolled. She had gone from the hospital to the home of someone in the Boston area, where she'd stayed for over a year. Her need to be "released" from that place had led her to call her friend in Barnard. He'd sent her bus ticket money, and there she was.

He asked if I could take her in. She was penniless. There was strong evidence that the woman near Boston with whom she'd lived had cashed the accident victim's annuity check the previous month, which was the only money she had to live on. She stayed with me for well over a month.

She had been married but now was divorced. She'd spent some six weeks in homeless shelters. She was articulate and trying to get her feet back under her. She represented what could happen to any of us if we fail to forge some kind of safety net.

Then there was the runaway — a true story about Christmas, Vermont and a runaway girl.

One year I had racked my brain for weeks before Christmas, wondering what special gifts to give my little girls, who were fast entering adolescence.

One evening after work I wandered through the Rutland Mall. Tucked in a corner was a vendor who had appeared for the holiday season only, selling small antique items and displaying lovely rings in a glass case.

I bought two rings, one with a small sapphire, the other with a ruby chip, both set in 10- or 14-carat gold. I don't remember which. The vendor was a pleasant lady who seemed as pleased as I that these rings, which she assured me were of good quality, would be the perfect gifts.

One ring fit; the other was too big. After Christmas I took the one that was too big to a Rutland jewelry store for sizing. A clerk looked at it and advised me that it wasn't worth his time to examine it, certainly not to size it. It wasn't a real stone, let alone a real chip.

A few days after Christmas, I lingered over a Saturday lunch in a Poultney café discussing with a friend an imminent move from our East Poultney home. Our lunch over, I returned home to resume packing.

Sitting among the boxes in the living room was a stranger, a girl who could have been fifteen or twenty-five, unkempt, wearing pants too big for her. She would have been a pretty girl if her hair were combed and if her clothes fit.

Her name was Sally, she said, and she had come to our house above the general store because a girl who used to live in town said we would help her. It seemed that she and her friend had ridden with truckers across the country. However, the friend, who looked younger than Sally, had been picked up as a runaway somewhere in the Midwest. That had left Sally, also a runaway, on her own to find her way to East Poultney.

How old was Sally? Eighteen, she said. And her last name? The truth was slow to come, but it turns out she was only fifteen, the adopted daughter, she said, of a sanitary engineer who lived somewhere in the mountains of southern California. She had everything, she said, a fact verified by her father who, when I called, told me he was a prominent citizen in town and that Sally had everything she could ever want. He couldn't understand why she would leave home, but he made no overtures to get her back.

Kittens had appeared on my doorstep before, but never a child. Despite her mature appearance, Sally was still a child. The question then was what to do with a child who didn't want to go home, whom I couldn't take with me to New York City, which was to be my family's new home, and who couldn't be sent packing, because that surely would mean returning to the truckers. I called a minister in town who agreed to meet with us in Rutland later in the week to search out a possible solution.

Now back to the rings. I had kept the card of the woman who sold me the rings. I told her that the rings we both had thought were "real" weren't and asked if she would take them back. She was upset and said the wholesaler who had sold them to her had misled her. She was sorry and would buy them back. We chatted. I told her about Sally. She told me that she and her husband had lost their only child, a daughter, just the year before, in an automobile accident. Could she see Sally? I told her I was meeting a minister in Rutland in a few days. Perhaps she would like to get a glimpse of Sally then.

The minister, Sally and I sat over coffee in the restaurant. The ring lady pulled up outside. On the pretense of returning the rings, which I did, I sat with her in the car, chatting, as she observed Sally and the minister inside.

The next day I met her again in Rutland, at her request. She had, it seems, discussed with her husband the possibility of taking Sally into their home. But her husband's grief was still too great to accommodate another child. She handed me an envelope. Inside were bills totaling $100 — to buy Sally some clothes, she said. This was a substantial sum in the early 1970s.

Sally and I went shopping. We bought Frye boots on sale, jeans, a blouse and a sweater, pausing for a lunch break at the Back Home Café, where Sally's eyes sparkled with excitement. How long had it been since she had had nice clothes and a pleasant meal in a place other than a truck stop?

She stayed with us until the actual moment we left Poultney. I left her with her new clothes at the minister's house. She would stay there for a few days before going to live with a Rutland family who wanted help caring for their young child. Sally lived there for a while, I understand, before moving on.

I haven't seen Sally or the ring lady since that week so long ago. But every year about this time I think of them both and of the little rings that brought us together. Were they so worthless after all, as the jeweler said?

Shelter for the guest who had suffered an automobile accident and for Sally had been offered because "There but for the grace of God go I," or someone I know.

Stray kittens continued to cross my path before I finally "got" that a beneficence shielding me from a guilty conscience may not in the long run be helpful to waifs and strays. Warmth, food and a clean bed benefited them only temporarily.

One day at the house in Montpelier, Vermont, the doorbell rang. A woman was selling vacuum cleaners. The Electrolux purchased to take care of vacuuming three floors of wall-to-wall carpeting was already a fixture. I didn't need what she was selling. In chatting with her I learned she was being asked to leave where she was living. She didn't have a home. She actually was sent to our door because someone (I never knew who) said, "Sara will take care of you."

I was working full time at the *Barre-Montpelier Times Argus*, a daily newspaper. I commuted just under an hour late afternoons and weekends to a ski resort near Burlington, Vermont, where I managed public relations projects. I was also freelance writing in a basement room next to the laundry room where, when the bells and whistles on the dryer sounded, I continued to type. My lack of concern for wrinkled clothes sitting in the dryer irritated my live-in companion, Joe, no end.

Be that as it may.

Would Vacuum Cleaner Lady assume the housekeeping duties here, were we to provide a room and meals? Yes, she would.

So far, so good. Theoretically this was a huge load off of me. She was more or less invisible — so much so, in fact, that after she spent weeks secluding herself in her bedroom, without having lifted a finger, Joe suggested he take her for a ride in the car. Where he deposited her, I never knew. We didn't lose a housekeeper. We lost a ghost and regained a guest room. Author Jim Harrison once wrote: "I'm always having a man in desperate straits trying to help somebody else out with no apparent success, because nobody can be helped by anybody."

Some months — maybe years — later, after harsh words were exchanged and the kind of damage inflicted that makes reconciliation improbable, I found myself living alone with my daughters in this house. My male companion, Joe, had moved out. Money was tight once again. In Montpelier, Vermont, members of the state legislature and other politicos often find rooms in local houses during the legislative session. Among the guests at my house was Jim Douglas, then serving as Vermont Secretary of State. He later would serve three terms as Vermont's governor. At the same time, another legislator and I became good friends while she was a paying guest at my house. We kept up our acquaintance until the advent of the Obama administration. Her vitriol against President Obama and her uber-far-right leanings led her to send me one-too-many emails full of political hate. Her notes died online but presaged for me the ugliness that's come to represent our national divide.

I prodded the house I eventually purchased in Barnard, Vermont, into a licensed bed-and-breakfast accommodation, thus monetizing my apparent penchant for allowing strangers into my home. Bed-and-breakfast guests linger for only a few nights. Long-term guests bring issues with them.

One thread appeared to unite the long-term waifs and strays. They all had difficult relationships with their mothers. One story was particularly heartbreaking. Gifts I was keeping for my daughters for Christmas, gifts still in their paper bags tucked under the linen shelf in the laundry room, caught the eye of this resident. One evening I came home to find her on her hands and knees, rummaging through these bags. This was not the best moment for either of us, and she left soon after, but not before tucking her own inferior-quality bed linens amongst mine and presumably taking off with a few of my own high-thread-count sheets.

To anyone with a penchant for pilfering, the owner of a bed-and-breakfast accommodation is the perfect stooge. The value of any pilfered item is always far below the $1,000 deductible, so it's pointless to report the thefts to the police and insurance company. Then came the day a longtime assistant at my bed and breakfast forged checks from my checkbook to pay for her opioid habit. Sadly, this led to her arrest, an act that (as she and I have subsequently discussed) probably saved her life. She never fell into the category of *Orange is the New Black* (a Netflix series exploring the lives of incarcerated women), but she came mighty close. Her mother is only now beginning to speak to me again. The hurt lingers.

Seats

I'd like to sit. Shall you sit too?
Then which chairs shall they be?
I was here until I stood and chanced to leave this seat.
So here shall be where I will sit,
leaving you to will your shall
in that chair across the way.
So be it.
If chairs arranged as they will be
suggest a conversation,
I'd like to chat.
Shall you chat too?

Rolling Stone

Someone famous once opined that five years in a job is more than long enough to learn all there is to know about the position — and maybe even about the company. I have probably averaged two years overall. My departures five years after my first assignment on a mountain and some years from the newspaper I loved were painful. The first was because I felt betrayed; the second didn't pay me enough to make ends meet. Bad luck? Good luck? Nobody kept score. Like the stone, I just kept rolling.

Throughout these journeys, with domiciles and bosses and desks constantly in flux, I could always count on my friends. One of these friends was an art therapist who became permanently disabled because her husband repeatedly beat her.

This dear friend, who died in 2007, was maid of honor at my wedding in 1960. We met during high school at 4-H Summer School, held annually on the Oregon State University campus in Corvallis. The school provided an opportunity for rural and urban youth to make new friends and to engage in leadership training.

How do we know why at age sixteen or seventeen we're drawn to a new friend? For me, someone who came from a tiny high school with a student body of only one hundred, meeting new people was a kind of miracle. She represented to me the sophistication of a large urban high school, where she had also been a leader. She had an excellent mind, was curious, loved to giggle and was exceptionally kind. She was a devout Catholic. I had been to her house, and she to mine.

Early on, I flexed my writing muscles and shared some of my thinking with her. She, in turn, was on the cusp of discovering what a fine artist she would someday be. I have some of her letters to me, and they are eloquent, sensitive and beautifully illustrated with her pen and ink sketches.

Fast forward. After my wedding, I didn't see her again until she visited the house where I lived with my young family in Portland, Oregon. She was married, having met her husband at a Catholic university in the Midwest. They were both officers of the Catholic Youth Organization at this school.

The years passed. In 1977 she wrote me a letter explaining that her husband, on their honeymoon, had begun beating her, a pattern that she tried to halt by going to a priest for advice. The priest told her to go home and take care of her family. Eventually there were four children. Her husband continued to beat her. Finally she and the children left him. There were at least two men after this who stepped in to help her. She married at least once again. But the damage both physical and emotional that she had endured was too much for these partners. They left. In a letter to me she wrote:

We looked to others as an ideally happy couple — and I tried hard ... all those years, I could never tell anyone, except a few "professionals" over the years ... I was a battered wife, Sara, I left A once in 1968 and took the boys to California and stayed with my friends ... I had left him a note that I would not return until a psychiatrist told me it was safe ... when I received one of many calls from the psychiatrist treating him. His judgement was that it was safe to return. Like a capital fool I did return.

It would be best to fill you in a bit and in some semblance of chronological order. After so many years of knowing him and our boxes of correspondence, I had become aware of the fact that his family life was far from happy — in fact, it was neurotic as hell! But I thought "love is blind," that those problems would not be ours ... actually we were moving away. A had been a battered child of sorts and in my presence always remained quiet, unattached toward his father. He was simply waiting for a scapegoat and I was it!

I was hit by him first on our honeymoon and beaten up for the first time two weeks after we were married. Friends came there from Oregon and I was in such anguish, and so confused about what I should do ... and there I was a Catholic — trapped forever — no divorce ... I almost asked them to take me back to Oregon with them, but I stayed on, soon learning I was expecting J. Then two weeks after J's birth we began graduate school ...

Then I lost a child (five months) between J and P, and we were for a time living in that little house you saw when you visited us, upon your return from Europe. There were not only beatings, but sexual abuse. I so often wandered off into the wee bit of Indiana woods that surrounded us and would sit weeping against one tree or another, wondering what to do. During that time, I promised myself not to have my spirit broken, [to hold on to] my love of life and love of learning. I kept that promise to myself, thank goodness!! For then I would have been the total victim.

Because A had no positive role model, fatherhood was hard for him. He was caught up in a real battle. He hated his father, yet he was constantly told by the church and American society that he must love his father. The schizoid behavior grew and grew, and there was a summer just as you had described with your husband where he was first admitted for care. But I couldn't get a doctor or psychiatric counseling service, etc., to respond as they did for you. They would only reply: 'He must come himself' no matter how severe my pleas — or badly bruised I was.

Finally, after the continuation of misuse, pain, sorrow — and then his always great sadness, begging forgiveness and promising me to give me no more mistreatment, and always begging me to promise my confidentiality — seven-and-a-half years married I began to pursue every effort to get him help. There would be periodic improvements — and then, if trouble, "Don't scream, the neighbors will hear." We would move. Usually he simply announced to me that we were moving.

She wrote that one of her four pregnancies was an incredible blow to her husband.

He went off the deep end. It is amazing this baby made it through the pregnancy with the difficulties we had, and there were many. I was so sad and working hard toward my degree, with him always terribly jealous of my successes.

After A's birth the beatings went completely out of hand, and walking in for help with my face a mess finally brought me success in seeking help.

I borrowed money from friends and left A a note and left for California … While standing tall and feeling free, what a joy to live without fear. I foolishly returned [in response] to his begging — and promises. He was going to continue psychiatric care when we moved to Michigan, and of course he refused to … Within three weeks I was expecting N … he didn't want me using birth control, and now I understand that when I was pregnant, I was trapped again.

By October (I returned in August) I was struck again for the first time [since coming back]. I should have packed up and moved out that night. But emotions are funny, aren't they. I was proud and also ashamed of the situation I was in and had been in, and of course I still could find enough good in him to love, and I hung on to hopes.

I doubt that there is anyone I know who can understand as well as you what all that is about. For your situation was much like mine. Only I do hope you weren't beaten too.

I was only struck once. This friend endured both physical and emotional beatings. I know well the anguish of living with a mentally ill person. Both her husband and my husband were mentally ill. Living with mental illness affects everyone in a household.

> *Then, as you know from my letters, for two years I faced five major surgeries (some directly related to injuries) … For a few days in April my sadness and bitterness over what a fool I'd been for so many years was very great. I will never be a normal person again — or at least not for many, many years. Their (the medical experts') goal just now is to hold off paralysis … the spinal specialist … told me that I had suffered severe soft tissue damage and it was all directly related to 15 years of beatings.*
>
> *How often I wanted to tell you what I was going through. To talk with you. As so often I would wonder how you and I … two young Oregon maidens, could have had such unnecessary unhappiness …*

One of her favorite quotes comes from Samuel Johnson: "That kind of life is most happy which affords us most opportunities of gaining our own esteem."

When I was working as a marketing director in New Hampshire, I sent her a plane ticket so she could fly in for a visit. At this time she and four children were subsisting on oatmeal three meals a day. She held advanced degrees in her newfound field, art therapy, and with one of her partners she published a book on the role of the arts in therapy, which was cutting edge at the time. While she was visiting, her daughter called me. I had never spoken with this daughter before. But she was asking for my help because she thought that her mother was drinking too much. And this daughter was right. The bottle of Scotch we stopped to purchase at the New Hampshire Liquor Store was the imperial quart. She carried it with her to her room every evening. By day, when I was at work, she seemed content to be painting. I treasure the Matisse-style still life she created over a few days and gave to me. When I commented that her hands were shaking and mentioned the call of concern from her daughter, she withdrew immediately. I had absolutely no experience with alcoholism. She may have perceived what I said as an intervention. The last few days of her visit were strained, with her commenting: "Guests, like fish, begin to smell after two days."

That was the last time I saw her. We did communicate again. When I called her at her home, she was living with a male friend who was of great assistance to her. By now the damage done to her when she was a bride and young mother had so eroded her spine that she could get in and out of bed only with a hoist. And she was in a wheelchair. But she painted and was active in both therapy and the arts in her community.

People wound others. And they themselves are wounded. Her spirit was indomitable, as was her faith, although I can't be sure about the latter toward the end of her life.

This friend and I each came from a household dominated by a patriarch. Each patriarch held his daughter to the old-fashioned values of virginity, modesty and duty. As daughters our best achievements were to be good and virtuous girls. It was years later that I cringed remembering the freshly baked cookies and lemonade I sometimes brought to my father while he was at work in a far pasture. Did I do this to further align myself with him or to show up my mother, who, by the time I was in my teens, had moved far away from trying to please her husband, or both? This pattern to please was established early on. When a man asked me to do something, I would turn over, like a dog on its back.

Searching High and Low

Some look high for leggy dames,
others low for girlish games.
Meanwhile countless lovely smiles
beckon through the aging miles.
Where's the man who cares to find
a woman with a seasoned mind
along with patience, years and girth
and possibilities for mirth?

Yoknapatawpha County

After saying good-bye to my childhood home when I married in 1960, I thought I had left behind small-town life forever. My high school graduating class in 1958 numbered eighteen. Gossip prevailed in Lowell, Oregon, long before the days of social media. Avoiding pregnancy and respecting authority and the Ten Commandments were imperatives to survival. After the stint at village life in East Poultney, I grew to love the anonymity that came with Manhattan, where I could reinvent myself over and over again, and no one was ever to know. However, I did not want to grow old and financially distressed in this city.

Thus I looked to tiny Barnard, population around nine hundred, to become my salvation. In the first few years I was a stranger in town, a position that allowed me, like the proverbial fly on the wall, to reflect on the people amongst whom I was now living. Unlike the stories of shoppers and their lives that were afforded me while standing behind the counter of the East Poultney General Store, the lives of the people in Barnard, at least those born and raised here and whose roots crouch sometimes eight generations deep in the rocky soil, fluttered by. Some years would pass before I, too, laid claim to a long-lived Vermont heritage, thanks to John R. Cobb, my many-times-removed great grandfather who probably drank ale with Ethan Allen and his boys during the Revolutionary War.

Who are my Barnard neighbors? Plumbers and handymen and house painters, gardeners and electricians, loggers, earth movers, carpenters and stone masons. Conversations asking them about their families move by fits and starts. Or talk can roam over the weather, the hay season and even the supply of firewood for the upcoming winter. If someone happens to be wearing a jacket emblazoned with Barnard Volunteer Fire Department, that's a good opener. Fundraising on behalf of the fire department is serious business in this small community, which throws its weight annually behind a flea market cum chicken barbecue held over there at Town Hall. Women in the Progressive Club are often the wives and mothers of the volunteers. They supply homemade pies to the barbecue, from which the scent of cooking chicken wafts a short distance to the Fan House.

Also supporting and participating in the theater of the community are doctors, retired professors, accountants, architects, librarians, retired CEOs, CIA spooks, and lawyers, along with artists who write children's books, play musical instruments and throw caution to the winds performing on stage.

Infrequent, however, are opportunities for offspring of the longest rooted to mingle socially with newcomers, those of us who, even after being in residence here for twenty years, may still be dubbed "flat-landers."

Perhaps I was expecting too much. I grew up in the 1940s and 1950s, in a farming and logging community in rural Oregon. If a new family came into the community, they were welcomed in by others. When I moved up here full time in late 2002, nary a soul said hello.

When ground was being readied for a new firehouse, large trucks filled with gravel shook my house as they sped to and from the work site. The speed limit here on Route 12 is thirty miles per hour. Sometimes drivers of these large trucks were hitting at least fifty miles per hour before they reached the four corners and had to downshift in order to make a sharp turn left onto North Road and continue to the construction site. I jumped in my car one morning around 8:30 and whipped up to the site. I spotted the truck that had just zoomed by my house and inched my car through the mud that lends its name to Mud Season in March and early April. I confronted the driver and told him I could tell by the RPMS (revolutions per minute) as he drove by that he was going way beyond the speed limit. He asked how I knew about RPMS and called me a "crazy old woman" and blew me off. Back in the car, my engine performed brilliantly as the wheels churned and charged and tunneled deeper and deeper into the mud. I was irrevocably stuck. Of course this story had a happy conclusion as far as the car was concerned. Someone called the man in charge of towing and I drove my car home. I suspect conversations at the construction site and maybe even among the volunteer firefighters themselves may have been enlivened for a while. I had become Barnard's token stuck-in-the-mud.

Farmers around here are a mix of young urban transplants and others who have bounced for decades with the fickle ways of the economy and Nature. Some have shifted from tending dairy cows to raising grass-fed cattle for beef. Vermont economic policies are stitched together with one goal — to protect what's called the working landscape. Agriculture plays into this by helping to secure open spaces. Farm produce delivered to my door includes free-range eggs and cheese, maple syrup, summer's bounty from the garden and in the cold months boxes of root vegetables, including way too many parsnips, which I've learned to share. The locavore movement is alive and well thanks to ambitious young people whose dedication to plow, plant and harvest gets a boost from interns called woofers (World Wide Opportunities on Organic Farms). Several of these young people joined my Thanksgiving table one year. I asked each how he or she had discovered Barnard, cynically assuming that trust funds may have allowed them to be here. One young woman said she was here to strengthen herself for the demands that being a citizen of the United States would ask of her. Trump and COVID-19 had not yet surfaced.

They created a CSA (community supported agriculture) happening that gathered on Thursdays from summer into October near the gardens. Upwards of four hundred people of assorted ages attend Feast & Field every week during the warm months. They enjoy farm-to-table food and live music that is sourced locally and internationally.

While Feast & Field's reach is legendary far beyond Barnard, few old-time locals venture up here on Thursday nights. Nobody ever speaks about a "town and gown" culture for fear of tipping a fragile balance. Town Meeting Day in March is the only time of year locals, who have lived here year-round for generations, and people like me, who will always be "flat-landers," congregate under one roof.

Some sons of these rooted generations star on football teams or dream of becoming a drummer in a band before donning the outdoor wear that marks investiture in the occupations of their fathers and uncles. Most often the work has to do with maneuvering large equipment. Daughters engage in painting their nails blue and comfort each other on Facebook when a boyfriend's eyes wander. The mother of one tribe was heard to say that she didn't want her children educated beyond high school because then they might want to leave her and move out of Vermont.

The state is perpetually lauded as one of the best places in the United

States for child-rearing families to live. Abundant opportunities for out-door recreation — snowshoeing, hiking, bicycling, skiing, and kayaking, for starters — woo many here. Snowmobiles and ATVs (all-terrain vehi-cles) symbolize the call of the wild before and after deer hunting season, which cascades weekly into seasons marked by bow and arrow, mus-ket and hunting rifle. Carcasses hang from makeshift gallows across the road from the Fan House. Young teenage daughters of two neighboring families each shot a deer one autumn. They stroked the heads of these wild beasts now resting in the backs of pickup trucks before the animals' lifeless bodies were strung up.

Is there a dictate that "thou shalt not cross the threshold?" BarnArts, a nonprofit community theater in Barnard, for years has tried to break through a barrier, as yet to be understood, that restrains these deeply rooted families from being part of an audience or a production. Yet an annual dinner to raise money for snowmobile recreation is always sold out. This is one event at which both town and gown chow down. My ex-perience at this event has been that conversations fail to flourish.

Town provides services that gown needs and in all reality can't ac-complish for themselves. But this symbiotic relationship is eroding as educated young people move into the community, willing to roll up their sleeves to mow lawns and vacuum houses. They market and price themselves differently from town, often convincing gown to pay more than gown is used to paying town. However these newcomers have en-ergy, they're cheerful, they return phone calls and they show up for work when they say they will. These attributes count for a lot in my bed and breakfast, where there are only hours between getting beds made and bathrooms cleaned before new guests arrive. Even the young man who has taken on walking my big white dog receives a healthy remunera-tion for each walk. The minimum hourly wage in Vermont as of 2022 is $12.55.

I'm unsure how much of what was once called Yankee ingenuity still flourishes in Barnard. But pecuniary interests do. Overheard at the Bar-nard General Store was a man bleating out (paraphrased): "When you work for Sara Widness, you can get any amount of money out of her that you want."

Whoa!

Overcharges? Work slow-downs? What was going on? He had accomplished many projects for me and was someone I trusted and respected. In fact, my daughter's wedding was going to be held at the Fan House, and just before this bit of commentary reached my ears, I had invited him to join the festivities. I do believe he was there that day. His work on my behalf stopped when I asked him just what he meant by the comment that had come my way. He was shamefaced. I was hurt.

On another occasion a young woman was doing some gardening for me. I was in the house when I tripped over a little gate that was keeping a small puppy out of the dining room. I fell backward with my Electrolux vacuum cleaner in my hand. The vacuum smashed down on a shin bone, and I gasped. I must have called out for help. The person in the garden came to see what had happened. I asked if she would please take me to the emergency room. She seemed to hesitate. I told her I would pay her hourly rate for the time she took to do this. We were off, the leg was cast. I paid her and never invited her back.

Keeping honest track of hours and expenses is, I thought (and still do), a gentleman's agreement. This agreement still does work. More important to me than being cheated of time or money, I am loathe to cheat myself of the belief, naïve though it may be, that people are intrinsically honest. Evidently the ice cutter tendency still prevails as I refuse to look over my shoulder to see who may be lying in wait to do me harm. I find life easier this way. However, when I am on the losing end of such a scenario, expunging the miscreant is the only card my scorn knows how to play.

Comme ça Chat

I sat in the angle of a late solstice sun as February lessened its taunt
in a winter that The Farmer's Almanac had predicted would be stern,
like one of those bearded Puritan preachers thumping on a pulpit
to assure all learn how to take the measure of hell or here
as wool-clad locals at the country store iterate
again and again and again what a winter this has been
with eight weeks left 'til May when, with luck,
not enough snow lingers under a top-down sun
to frost a margarita glass for Cinco de Mayo.

Biding My Time

Perching myself permanently and finally, so it appears, in Vermont bought me time. And along with time, I can think. Without time, thinking, for me, ceases. As professionals, we may think we're thinking as we react in ways we've been trained and instructed to react. This isn't thinking as is the friend I've come to embrace in solitude here. However, thinking doesn't necessarily pay the bills. Managing a bed and breakfast, freelance writing and being part of a small consultancy, Widness & Wiggins Public Relations, together help balance the checkbook and provide satisfactions.

Sometimes all three worlds beg for attention at the same time. A client emails and needs an answer now. An editor has a question about a story I just submitted. The bed and breakfast guests are coming down to breakfast and, if I am lucky, companions are presenting themselves together, because if the man leaves the wife sleeping upstairs, he usually positions himself on a stool at my kitchen counter and tells me stories about the new warehouse he just built or that his grandfather was a governor of such-and-such a state. Am I interested? Of course. Can I multitask at 7:30 in the morning with Mr. Motor Mouth going full steam in front of me? Barely. These moments can be challenging.

Since early 2003, when I received a license from the State of Vermont to operate a bed and breakfast in the Green Mountains, I have received hundreds of guests from all over the world. Few are here on business. Most come to enjoy for a few brief hours an endangered landscape that is a balm for the soul.

As an experienced traveler who once guided journalists around the world, I have a sixth sense about what people may enjoy and try to steer them accordingly. Rarely do people have enough time to take the canoe onto Silver Lake or to hike the Appalachian Trail. Some, unused to dark night skies, wonder why they're here. Others want to know where to shop. Always I try to guide people to the most reliable dining venues. If they don't enjoy their dinners while they are staying here, then their Fan House experience may be tainted.

As long as I am organized, breakfasts are fun. Usually every table of newcomers gets the Sara spiel about Barnard, about Vermont, about this state's environmental commitment and so on. Guests depart for the day with more than pancakes. As with shipboard friendships, guests appear to bond over the breakfast table. Whether or not these newfound friends continue on to Christmas-card status, I don't know. But I enjoy facilitating such possibilities.

German-speaking visitors are often in Barnard for the same reason that some of us might make a pilgrimage to Stratford-upon-Avon. A German writer, Carl Zuckmayer, a playwright with a strong political bent, and his wife, Alice, lived in Barnard for several years during World War II. They had been encouraged by journalist Dorothy Thompson to share life in this little village with her. Dorothy and the Pulitzer Prize–winning author Sinclair Lewis, her husband, lived at Twin Farms, today a five-star resort, just a mile up the road from the Fan House. Alice Herdan-Zuckmayer wrote of their time here in her book, *The Farm in the Green Mountains*. Although the house, now owned by the Kahn family, isn't open to the public, with advance notice a family member is happy to show a visitor through the dwelling little-changed since it was built in the early 1780s. Sometimes these visitors stay at the Fan House. A friend who has created a short documentary on Dorothy Thompson often joins the breakfast table to shed scholarly insight into the challenges life in Barnard presented Dorothy Thompson and assorted intellectuals dispossessed of their own careers and expectations by the events of World War II. A first rule of thumb the locals laid down to Dorothy was that everyone went on a first-name basis and nobody was to be considered anybody else's servant.

The Zuckmayer farm drew a gentleman from Switzerland into my house one summer afternoon. Someone at the Barnard General Store had told him that I might be able to help him see the property. He knocked on my door. We got into my car and I was able to give him a glimpse of the old Zuckmayer farm, where hospitality had presided when, among others, playwright Bertolt Brecht visited. Brecht would have been surrounded by the cacophony of chickens that helped support the Zuckmayers or, most certainly in early September, a chorus of crickets. We returned to my house for tea. I think we might have been conversing in German and he may have told me more than I was able to grasp with my limited ability in this language. He was sipping his tea through tears because he was so overwhelmed at having completed a pilgrimage that was important to his own family. This man's story left with him, although the memory of his visit lingers.

Time for Music

Time for my friend who calls from afar
'tho my coat is buttoned and the door's ajar;
time for the blue jays out there in the snow
who expect to be fed when it's 20 below;
time for the fire that refuses to light
until ashes are cleaned and the kindling's just right;
time for the music ...

Politics and Pedants

Today at the post office while I was mailing a package, a neighbor of a particularly ardent political persuasion stood behind me. A young girl came in to pick up a parcel far too big for her to carry. Was someone coming for her? She was uncertain. He offered to take her and the package to her house. She hesitated and rightly so. I suggested that if she preferred not to ride with a strange man I would be happy to take her and her package to her house. The neighbor seemed surprised but then realized the wisdom of my gesture. A few minutes later a strange woman came in looking for directions. He provided her the information she needed to get where she thought she wanted to go. I suggested to the neighbor that he stand out in the street with a sandwich board stating "Information and help dispensed here." These encounters occurred in the dark days — for some — following the 2016 presidential election and the baring of Republican teeth in the House and Senate as elected officials prepared to gnaw to the bone any semblance of safety net in this country. Before driving away, I should have suggested he wear a signboard messaging "Care for the heavy laden, Help to immigrants and overall Succor to the common man." He's bright. He would understand where I am coming from. But there was no room for banter in my heavy heart. I was not alone.

This same neighbor a few years earlier was speaking with my nephew, again in the post office. When the nephew mentioned that Sara was his aunt, the neighbor charged that I was a Communist because he had seen me pick up my mail that included a brochure from Acorn. His ACORN is an acronym for the Association of Community Organizations for Reform Now. My Acorn is a brochure promoting DVDs, mostly British, and HRH-themed gift items. The next time I received an Acorn brochure, I asked the postmistress to put it in this neighbor's box. When next I ran into him, I asked if he enjoyed the brochure.

Chappy the Big White Dog is well-known to this tiny town for several reasons. First, I am always looking for someone to walk his ninety-five pounds because even though I weigh more than the dog does, I don't want to break any bones when a chipmunk catches his eye. Chappy is surprisingly light on his feet; so light, in fact, that when he pirouettes at the kitchen door after coming in off the porch en route to his dog dish, only about two square feet of century-plus-old pine floor is scratched. Second, he is a rescue dog from a kill shelter in Alabama, deposited along with assorted canine friends in a motel parking lot in White River Junction, Vermont, after being crated and transported from Dixieland. The rescue dogs emerged from the freight truck, walked down the ramp and lunged into the protective arms of their new adoptive Yankee families. This is what Chappy did in the summer of 2012, purportedly as my daughter's dog, but through complications too various to explain here, he nudged his way over to my house. Because he is a rescue dog, connecting the possibly horrific dots of his life before he came to Vermont is relatively easy. Think underpaid workers in uniforms resembling those of the UPS or Fed Ex drivers, wearing hats, just as the drivers do, but without the friendly faces that emerge from delivery vans. These underpaid workers scolded and perhaps even beat the poor animals, whose only hope for the next bowl of kibble rests in their adoptive parents. Let's just say that there may have been some bad chemistry going on in Chappy's past life. Delivery people elicit a close-to-foamy response and more if they fail to honk before they come down the driveway and if I don't get to their truck before Chappy does. Also, he is some kind of herding variety and likes to roam and bolt into and run through woods and wide-open spaces. Several nearby neighbors have recently added chicken inventories to their gardens. Chappy discovered one such garden one fateful day and terrorized a chicken named Squirty. The chicken died. I wrote a card, brought over a memorial gift and a restitution check and have since collected the neighbor's phone number so I can urgently call when Chappy gets loose again.

Playing with Feathers

Whenever people flock together
we wonder if we're all a feather,
probing drafts that come our way
when all we want to do is play.

Trick or Treat

New Year's Eve 2017 at the Fan House rings with the laughter of bed-and-breakfast guests from the South. This family reveal themselves as libertarians and Trump supporters: grandparents devoted to their family and to their hometown university; daughter-in-law/mother of three children, happy to have been a stay-at-home mom; eldest grand-daughter, in her early twenties, already indoctrinated against liberals; youngest granddaughter, moving through life in mission and outreach work while still in a Christian high school; creative grandson, inarticu-late, confused and trending liberal in a highly conservative household; and the children's father, son of conservatives, doing a juggling act and seeming tense.

I listen to discourse between them and another couple, conservatives from Vermont, discussing the merits of change for change's sake and how great the new Trump administration will be. Find myself unable to breathe in my own living room, in front of my own fireplace. Under any circumstance, as hostess I am constrained from articulating anything I am thinking while understanding immediately how quickly PC (politi-cal correctness) comes into effect. I am aware that I must be very aware of what is happening to me, of how I am reacting by not reacting.

Breakfast conversation with conservative Vermonters and liberal guests — after family from the South leaves — hovers over the need to try to understand where the other person is coming from. The question posed is: "We're all the same, aren't we?"

I can only make a difference, and perhaps only to myself, by listening and trying to understand.

The Blue March

Forget-me-nots marched on my lawn today,
laying a swath of blue.
Minute by minute their tribute increased
as bands of color grew.

Pondering Roots

Efforts to dodge the nonsense that can derail the enjoyment of living in a rural village opened my pathways to introspection. Although still the girl on the prow, I find challenging the risks of waves — any kind of waves — less appealing in my eighties.

Fully two decades after the tsunami that shuttered my New York public relations agency, my new hobby, genealogy, hinted at what might have gone amiss. My former business partner and I undoubtedly share a bloodline that goes back at least to circa 1400 and a Lady So-and-So of Cornwall. She is only the first of the purported ancestors I've found who bear this family's name, a family to which I am related. Perhaps our joining forces for a short while in Manhattan was an acting out of centuries-old karma.

I am having an amazing time with Ancestry. One day I traced my maiden name, Duncan, back to the 1300s, through direct ancestry lines, including what are called "thrulines," as result of Ancestry DNA tests. I am intrigued by the thought that my family may go back to the Picts, known as the painted people. Do the peoples of our pasts matter? I feel as if I have one hundred grandmothers sitting on my shoulders and telling me to be a good girl. Are you serious? Only one glass of wine in front of the fire tonight?

Pursuing genealogy through Ancestry.com is quite a bit like putting coins in a slot machine, with jackpots of various sizes accumulating. I've hit the jackpot several times when it comes to sourcing relatives I never knew I had. Both of my parents were only children. When my grandparents died, so did the family embroidery, the stories, that multiple generations share. My ancestors were a mystery to me until through Ancestry I met a cousin who lives in Virginia. Our several-times-removed great-grandfathers were brothers. My great-grandfather stepped up to the plate to help his brother's family when the brother died at Manassas, in the Civil War. We first met at the Inn at Willow Grove, in Orange, Virginia, just sixty-three miles from Manassas. She and her husband have visited me in Vermont and met my daughters.

Another cousin who has visited me is a several-times-removed great-grandchild, as am I, of John Reed Cobb, who lived in Vermont, in the towns of Charlotte and Clarendon, before and after the Revolutionary War. Thanks to a connection made through Ancestry, this cousin introduced himself one summer and shared family lore and photos of the Cobb family.

Unbeknownst to me while growing up on the farm in Lane County, Oregon, a few hours up the road, in Portland, lived Roxanne, the daughter of my mother's first cousin, a professor at the University of Nevada at Reno. I never did meet her, but one of her sons and a granddaughter visited the Fan House when we connected through Ancestry.

A New Zealand cousin on my father's side has shared extensive material about my paternal grandmother's family, the Wraggs, who lived a colorful life in Leeds. A UK cousin who lives in Kent shared a photo of a tartan-clad Duncan cousin from Ayrshire.

Through a connection with Doug Heath, historian for the Drummond family of Scotland, I have photos of a great aunt, Jean Bone Duncan, who married a Drummond. Doug also invited me and my brothers to affiliate with the Drummond clan.

The discoveries continue.

However, as interesting to me as my newfound cousins are, so too are psychic connections I have experienced in places where forebears once breathed.

Before I came to know about these characters, I had sensed, for example, presences in Culpepper, Virginia. Turns out that this is the region where some of my uncles and cousins fled after their father, a minister, was beheaded in Scotland. The Scots were among the first people to settle the early South. They brought with them a distrust for power that continues today. As I write this there are a disproportionate number of politicos with Scottish surnames sitting in southern and national seats of power. Their forebears left miles of stone walls behind them in the old country. Sometimes a genetic coding seems to assert itself when it comes to their stonewalling of compassion and reality.

I was led kicking and screaming to a state of almost-retirement due to the onslaught of the 2020–2021 pandemic, which resulted in a steep decline in bed-and-breakfast reservations and the almost complete demise of Widness & Wiggins Public Relations. However, I have had more time to indulge my hobby and near passion. This week I have hovered over Ancestry, which reveals an extensive collection of apparently lusty and highly fertile Scotsmen who seemed to have had more than enough time to produce scores of offspring. It didn't take long for some of the sons to get out of Dodge, where "the clearances" disallowed them a living on Scottish lands and where anyone who was no longer a Catholic stood a chance of losing their head.

So, what's a man to do? Hightail it to the Promised Land and especially to the South, where new arrivals brought with them the scars and maybe even the muscle memory that we think may be carried in mother's milk. Then slip into the whiskey a genetic coding that perhaps comes down through this clan-driven culture who were "disinherited" by the chieftains, after centuries of being called up to go to war in yet another skirmish with the English. Historically these lairds had valued their clansmen as warriors and fighters. But for nearly one hundred years, between the mid-18th century and mid-19th century, landowners sent their tenant farmers and families packing in order to free up lands for grazing sheep. This displacement was a blow to many of these people, who a century before had fought for the right for religious freedom. They wanted to be Protestants.

Many of the new arrivals in America were Scots-Irish, people from the Ulster Plantation of Ireland, which began in the early 17th century to offload onto the Emerald Isle populations of Scots and English who spoke English and were Protestant. These newcomers to Ireland, who took over lands worked by Gaelic-speaking Catholics, didn't have much choice in the matter; it was a policy implemented by James I of England to try to balance the linguistic and religious playing field in Ireland. The perception was that the Catholic and Gaelic-speaking Irish posed a threat to the English crown through potential liaisons with other Catholic countries and enemies of the English crown. These transplants from northern England and Scotland were among those starved and died during the 19th-century famines in Ireland.

In Scotland, those bereft of lands to farm thanks to some one hundred years of the Highland Clearances flocked to the southern United States.

(The Clearances essentially kicked tenant families off of lands they had lived on and worked for centuries so that the lairds would have more room to pasture sheep for the burgeoning textile industry.) Many others who came to America had been exiled as political and other types of prisoners. Even indentured servants who arrived in America with their owners could in the foreseeable future own their own land. New arrivals who'd left families of substance behind them in Scotland and had coins to jingle in their pockets could purchase slaves to help them farm vast acreages of tobacco, sugar cane, cotton and indigo. Eventually, freed indentured servants would climb on the backs of others to further their own ends.

Now fast-forward to Senators Lindsay Graham, Mitch McConnell, Richard Burr, Rick Scott and John Kennedy, all with burrs and lilts hovering around their surnames if not their genes. They're all in the South. Why would anyone expect that with the genetic coding that may be rampant in their blood that they will suddenly evolve into caring and compassionate human beings when it may be highly likely (too much research entailed to prove conclusively) that they are how they are because way back their forebears crawled on the backs of others to get where they stand today. I know this can be conceived as a gross assumption, but I am stating this to make a point. If ever history is important, it's important now, more than ever, so that collectively we can begin to understand how and why we're in this many-pronged crisis: cultural recidivism, global warming, drought and a simmering civil war, to name a few of those prongs.

Humiliations, physical scars of abuse, hunger, poverty and despair… So many people are still riding on the backs of others who experience some or all of these atrocities on a daily basis.

When recently I was compelled to go to a hardware store, I had two choices: I could shop at a smaller, closer-to-home store or at the one that is larger but farther away. The closer-to-home store has a relatively new owner. Since he took over, the store has been selling ammunition and gun-related items. My current state of mind being what it is, I thought: *Do I want to go to an establishment that probably is being run by a member of the NRA (National Rifle Association)?* Efficiencies of locale, however, prevailed. I was the only customer in the store. I asked the owner: "I know you sell ammunition; are you a member of the NRA? What are your thoughts on possibilities that the NRA filtered Russian funds for Trump's election? Have you been receiving NRA communiques on this alleged situation?" He said: "When I applied for the licenses I needed to sell ammunition for hunting rifles, I was solicited by the NRA to join them. No, I am not a member of the NRA." We exchanged a few collegial clucks about the horrific state of affairs and I left. My point: I had gone in armed for bear; I was disarmed by his honesty. And I need to constantly remind myself to check attitude and assumptions at the door.

Just as Culpepper, Virginia, had stirred my connections with my roots, so did Warwick Castle near Stratford-on-Avon, and such long-ago British empires as New Delhi and, in Burma, Bagan. I have an instinctive habit when walking through ancient stone- and brick-lined passageways; I hold my hands palms out, seeking energies emanating from the walls of medieval fortresses and Buddhist temples. I could not control my tears in a cemetery in Charleston, South Carolina. Such incidents of weeping also happened on several Caribbean islands, one of which might have been where Andrew (Duncan) McDonald lived. This first cousin left my father an inheritance.

Past lives have washed over me so many times. The familiar can be a place or simply an unexpected synergy that I experience with a colleague or friend who, as I discover only years later, shares a surname on my family tree. The coincidences are too many to recount. Thank goodness I didn't know about all of these forebears when I was traveling through Europe. Instead of enjoying sidewalk cafes, I would have been searching for the next bronze plaque on yet another marble or stone effigy on top of or buried under those countless and always-cold cathedral floors. These past lives that tumble before us perhaps account for déjà vu.

On one Halloween Eve, years after a U-Haul deposited my New York office and life at the Fan House doorstep, I knew my world had shifted. The young energy at the Barnard General Store organized the neighborhood to receive trick or treaters. At the Fan House they would find an old lady in a long black dress covered by a white bib apron. A black scarf covered her head and shoulders. However, I was fearful that a broom would unsettle youngsters, who might truly believe I was a witch, a reputation that would doubtless go with me to my grave in Barnard. I loved seeing the children and their parents. I loved being in costume and in the moment. I was engaging with children as I used to when I was a young mother — in a spirit of playfulness and fun.

My true roots, however, vestiges of those Puritan leftovers, those shadows that brand me as a daughter of the *Mayflower*, were on display that night at the Fan House. Children could help themselves to treats from one bag full of candy and a second bag full of little boxes of raisins. I offered raisins out of respect for the parents who believe that living healthy lives close to the earth, as they do here, will save the future for their children. I believe this too.

A Survey Map

*Without the smile the creases sit
right atop my upper lip.
With the smile the rivers glide
around the mouth on either side.
The net result, it must be said,
is survey maps around my head,
topographical at best,
gleaned from life's ongoing quest*

Thank Yous

Heartfelt thanks to Margaret Edwards whose popular memoir classes in Woodstock, Vermont, challenged me to stay the course with this manuscript. Thanks, too, to book club mates. Brad Wetzler saved my sanity and Dianna Delling's careful copy edits saved this book. Thank you Jennifer Steedly, Anne Shafmaster and Geza Tatrallyay for your close reading. Gary Miller persuaded me to get out of my comfort zone and dig into how things truly felt. Frank Gado reminded me that life is in the details. Kudos to Kitty Werner for helping guide my book to the bookshelf!